A Touch
of Greatness

A Touch
of Greatness

by

Harold E. Kohn

Illustrated by the Author

WILLIAM B. EERDMANS PUBLISHING COMPANY
GRAND RAPIDS, MICHIGAN

To
my brother and sisters,
Alvin, Gildreth and Shirley,
with
affection
and
gratitude

Foreword

Who are the great? Those who possess the most political or economic power? The best known, the eminent? Hardly. This may be the world's way of defining greatness. But long ago Jesus said, "Whoever would be great among you must be your servant." In the Greek the word used for "servant" meant "slave." Think of the truly great of all time. Were they not under bond of conscience, bound by a sense of responsibility and obligation toward world need, near and far, and toward God?

The great are always slaves, mastered by the urge to help. Often they serve in secret ways, without salary, status or recognition. One man I know sends assistance to children in a needy family by devious channels so that they cannot discover the name of their benefactor. Another "moonlights" on a second job each day when his first job is done, so that his son can attend college. No task is too humble for the great, as was the case with a scrub woman who financed a long, expensive and discouraging pursuit of justice that at last freed her wrongfully imprisoned boy.

Between these covers the reader will not find detailed biography. Instead, the book presents glimpses of the great, here a revealing incident or anecdote and there a word of wisdom spoken by some servant of mankind. The title reminds us that greatness does not come in large, solid ingots, like the giant bars of gold kept safe in Fort Knox. Rather, we find touches of glory appearing in imperfect lives. No one mentioned in this book was so thoroughly great in every respect that no flaw of self-service ever marred him, excepting One who, even when He stoops to serve, stands tall above all others in the perfection of selfless love.

In days of turmoil, tension and testing, every sensitive, responsible person seeks guidance on how to live the good life of service, and hence how to be great in small ways, where he is, with what he has, right now — by God's grace. We seek an ageless wisdom, mellowed in time and appropriate to our generation. These essays are published in the hope that some qualities of life found in great persons, famed or obscure, may excite the imagination of the reader and inspire him as they have inspired the author.

Hidden heroes daily bless the world with great words quietly spoken, great burdens silently lifted, great deeds of mercy and kindness secretly performed. Perhaps some word of faith found here may call others to join those who have dwelt under the same skies that cover us and have walked the same earth as we, leaving a bit of glory in their paths and "a touch of greatness" upon their times.

I express hearty appreciation to S. George Little, President and Executive Editor of General Features Corporation, and to his staff, for unfailing kindnesses to me and for permission to print in this book several of my essays previously published by General Features. Several articles included here were published in the *Charlevoix Courier*. Hearty thanks are hereby offered to the editor Harold Totten for his helpfulness. My gratitude is here expressed to my daughter Carolyn Kohn Minch and to Mrs. LaVerne Heise, who have typed manuscript, and to my wife Marian, who has read proof with generous help and encouragement.

And to the innumerable good people who have unwittingly blessed me with their gentle grace, simple wisdom and quiet example I offer my profound and lasting thanks.

Contents

1

Life's Climate Is More Important Than Its Weather

The difference between weather and climate is mostly a matter of time. Weather is momentary. Climate endures. Weather may fluctuate wildly, as it does in springtime throughout much of North America. One day is humid, followed by rain. Then comes a high wind that dries off the earth, and we enjoy several days of bright sunshine. Soon clouds return; the high temperature drops, and more silvery rain slants down from leaden heavens. Weather is a temporary occurrence of any of its various components such as humidity, cloudiness, precipitation, rising or dropping pressure, temperature or wind.

Climate, on the other hand, is not an instantaneous occurrence, but a long, enduring, prevailing characteristic of any of these components. It is a pattern or design of conditions that have existed over an area for a long time. It is climate rather than weather that determines what plants, insects, birds and mammals can grow in a

11

region. Climate, more than weather, has helped mold civilizations. Although the Temperate Zone of the world, in which we live, is often affected by the worst possible weather such as tornadoes or hurricanes and tempests of stupendous force, the world's most highly developed civiliations are found in the Temperate Zone, because here the climate is neither too hot nor too cold to do the work that makes for progress and because here there is enough variation of weather components to invigorate the body and stimulate the mind.

The best climate can occasionally be assaulted with the worst weather. Even the sunny Bahamas are sometimes assailed by hurricanes.

The soul, too, experiences both climate and weather. There is a sum total of the soul's condition, its convictions, courage and hopes, its moral purposes, its sense of justice and mercy. These make for a "good climate." Or the soul may suffer from "poor climate" where prevailing conditions consist of hostilities, grudgefulness, deceitfulness, ingratitude, immorality, anxiety.

Then, again, there is the condition that predominates at any given moment of time, the soul's weather, its moods.

In the Forty-second Psalm a comparison is made between spiritual weather and climate: "Why art thou cast down, O my soul? And why art thou disquieted within me? Hope thou in God; for I shall yet praise him." For the time being the Psalmist is depressed. He experiences heavy skies and stormy spiritual weather. Nevertheless, he lives in a climate of trust, hope and joy. He knows bad weather will pass and good climate will remain. Depression and disquietude are his weather. Hope and joy are his climate. He refuses to confuse the two.

How can we best handle life's changing weather, its fluctuating moods?

First, remember that troublesome moods are universal. Glandular, metabolic or blood-pressure changes make emotional differences in everyone. So do the frustrations or good fortune, the failures or successes life brings to us. Everyone everywhere normally experiences moods, as every spot on earth undergoes some changes in the weather.

Secondly, keep in mind that the mood will not last forever. Moods come and go as do rainy days. While we are in the midst of a foul mood it appears to us to be permanent. But so did the last mood, as did the one before that and all of its countless predecessors. This one, too, will soon be gone. In his youth and middle years Abraham Lincoln frequently became so depressed that his friends despaired of his sanity and of his life. One way he learned to handle his low moods was by expecting them to arrive before they came and by expecting them to leave soon after they overtook him. He was often heard to quote from a poem the last line of which read, "This will pass away." A mood is as transitory as a sunshine-filled day or as a rainstorm. Our elation and depression appear permanent, but we have passed from happiness to disconsolation and back to happiness again, repeatedly. And it will happen again. Expect a change in moods; then, when it comes, it will be less disturbing.

Thirdly, do something worthwhile in the meantime, until the mood passes. One woman says she goes shopping for a hat when a stubborn cloud of gloom refuses to move away. A new red hat in particular dispels depression, she declares. Probably the mood would pass as quickly without her purchasing a hat, but looking for a suitable hat gives her something to do in the meantime.

A housewife testifies that baking bread helps her moods. She feels she is performing a fundamental task and putting her competence to work. By the time the bread is a fragrant brown her spirits are refreshed.

Take a walk. Hoe the garden in summer, or shovel a path in winter. Visit a friend. Do something while the mood passes.

Fourthly, refuse to give your moods more importance than they deserve. Many things matter more than whether we *feel* "blue" or sunny, irritable or patient, upset or serene. The happiness of those around us is of more account than our moods. Why should we vent our irritability on children who may be innocent of wrongdoing, or make the family miserable with our inner distress — spreading suffering with our inconsideration, quarrelsomeness, criticism or sullenness. Hitler, who almost worshiped his moods, declared, "I think with my blood!" Indeed he did, and thus precipitated the bloodiest era in history. Whenever emotions run amuck they cause anguish. No matter how we feel, the happiness and welfare of others still count. Show it.

When we treat our moods as important, then they become far *too* important. Attach little importance to how you feel at the moment.

Fifthly, bear in mind that moods are untrustworthy guides to reality or to conduct. We do not see the world as it is, but we see it through what we are. Moods strain the outside world with the color of our emotion. When we are glad and gay the world seems more trouble-free than it actually is; it takes on the glow of our lively mood. When we feel hopeless, the world looks bleak and empty. When we feel lonesome, the world appears to be hardhearted and uncaring. Moods discolor our view of the world.

Moreover, if followed, bad moods would misguide us into wrong conduct. If everyone acted exactly the way he felt, the number of desertions, assaults, killings and suicides would multiply immeasurably. If everyone worked only when he was in the mood, the world's work would grind to a halt in quick order. Only the highest ideals are clear enough windows through which to view the world, and only the best principles make worthy guides of conduct. The Psalmist knew he could trust his convictions concerning God's goodness, but not his changeable feelings.

Sixthly, drain off excess emotion into good works. Poised people often get as angry as the rest of us, but they do not thrash out at those nearest them with hard blows or harsh words. Instead they undertake some constructive activity, fixing furniture, building a birdhouse, picking flowers and taking them to a shut-in. A man of my acquaintance says he keeps his spirit from going lopsided under the weight of a chronic physical affliction by the technique of carrying someone else's load of trouble, along with his own. He declares trouble is like a burdensome suitcase: carry it with one hand and it almost tips a person over. Pick up another's suitcase in the other hand and carry it for him, and it is possible to walk upright. Another's trouble balances one's own. Good works help bad moods. Tell your excess emotions where to go — into good deeds.

Finally, a healthy measure of emotional control can be gained by attaching one's feelings to appropriate objects. Misspent emotions represent one of the world's most tragic wastes. "Good emotions" should not be spent on soggy sentimentalism. Pity, sympathy and love should find a fitting expression. William James once told of a Russian coachman who was compelled to remain in his coach, freezing, while his wealthy employer sat at the opera weeping at the tragic fate of the operatic hero. She delighted in sensing fictional sorrows while ignoring real hardships she was causing and which she could alleviate. Dr. James declared we should *do* something with our good feelings which are aroused through drama, poetry, art, music, or religion: tip the waiter a bit extra; buy your wife that longed-for hat; say a kind word to your mother-in-law. Hate what is really hateful — diseases, poverty, wars that destroy men's bodies, and all the influences that destroy men's souls. Love the lovely, in nature, in man, in the fine arts. Especially, "Thou shalt love the Lord thy God with all thine heart, and with all thy soul, and with all thy might."

Then put the emotion into an appropriate action. Destroy the destructive. Give support to the good. Help the helpless. Work for the reign of God in all human affairs. Emotions and motions go together.

2

We Are Here to Be Spent

Sacrifice, like gravity, is built into the structure of the universe.

All life exists at the expense of other life. You will be able to eat your next meal because some creature has died. All dishes of meat, fowl or fish represent the sacrifice of one life that your life might be sustained. A slice of bread is made of grain that once grew in a field, nurtured by life forces in the soil, bathed by the sun, drinking of the rains. Grain dies that man might live. From microscopic amoeba to man, this rule runs like a scarlet thread through the tapestry of nature: all life is sustained through the sacrifice of other life.

Voluntary sacrifice has a conspicuous place in the world's religions. The ancient Hebrews offered the first fruits of their harvests and the best animals of their flocks and herds in penitence for sin and in thanksgiving for God's blessings. Romans made a libation of wine to their gods. Brahmins offered sacrifices of horses. Bulls were

18

slaughtered as sacrifices to the Persian god of light, Mithra, the defender of truth and enemy of the powers of darkness. The Maoris and the Aztecs were among the many people who made human sacrifices to their gods. Christians believe the slaying of Jesus Christ on the cross was the Supreme Sacrifice made for the forgiveness of sins and for reconciling wayward man to God.

What is behind sacrifice? What does sacrifice mean? In secular terms a sacrifice may simply represent a loss, as when a beef steer must lose its life that man may enjoy steaks and roasts. But "sacrifice" has higher, holier meanings. The word itself comes from two Latin words meaning "sacred" and "to make." In religious terms a sacrifice is anything that is dedicated to a divine being, thus taking on a sacred significance.

In the lowest forms of primitive religion sacrifices were attempts to appease the anger of gods who were offended at man's transgressions, or they were endeavors to bribe the gods to do favors for man. But in the Hebrew faith and in Christian practice sacrifices are ways of returning to God the life God gave to men. Whether it is a lamb slain on an altar or money placed in an offering plate, a sacrifice is man's acknowledgment that his life is not his own. It is God's life. Man's body and breath, mind and spirit; man's sheep and cattle, land and gold; and man's dear ones, too, are loaned to him for a while. All religious sacrifices of a high order are but outward symbols of this essential truth that the universe and all things in it are God's to be used for God's purposes.

One of the major transformations of the human spirit comes when a person makes the move from infantile egocentricity, where everything is "mine," to be used for "my" comfort and pleasure and satisfaction, to that position where everything is God's, to be used for God's purposes and for man's good. In the child's world attention is focused on "my bottle," "my blocks," "my tricycle." In the spiritually mature person this is God's world; people are God's children; every event is God's affair. Attention is shifted from self to God and to other people. This change makes joyous, sacrificial living possible.

When this conversion occurs a person is ready to accept risks of pain and death for the sake of others and for God's sake. He can do this because, unlike the self-centered person, he feels the world is more important than his own little concerns, and that the world will not fall apart if pain, tragedy or death should visit him. He is God's as everything else is God's. He is not here to be spared but to be spent. If he must give his energy, time, money, or life for the sake of the common good and for God's sake, he has the conviction he is doing right because he belongs to God and God's children anyway, and not to himself.

The great sacrifices of history have made human progress possible. Countless known and unknown heroes of the race have grandly, audaciously, sacramentally laid down their lives for the sake of some cause more important than themselves. They became absorbed in a great purpose, and their love expressed itself in sacrifice. Peter and Paul lived and died sacrificially. So did Father Damien, missionary to lepers. So did Dr. Barlow, who deliberately swallowed the germs of a Chinese pestilence and then rushed to Johns Hopkins Medical School to be studied so that the causes of the plague might be known and fought by medical science.

Many years ago a Chinese Christian police official was ordered by his superiors to rid a certain Pacific island of pagan tribal customs. He was to attack head-hunting first. He accomplished nothing by simply ordering the islanders to abandon the practice of head-hunting. Punishment only made the natives rebellious and more determined than ever to take the heads of their enemies as trophies. The natives gradually grew fond of the Chinese official and at last came to love him. They noticed that whenever they performed their gruesome murder ritual their Chinese friend became very sad for many days. His grief troubled them, and they promised they would never again go head-hunting. But they broke their promise.

At last their Chinese friend told the head-hunters to make no more promises to quit their evil practice. Then he astounded them by announcing that, since they had failed to break their evil habit, he had decided to join them in it. To demonstrate his earnestness he would tell them where to find the next victim to be murdered. On a given night the victim would be discovered sleeping, wrapped in a red blanket and lying in a certain corner of the forest.

The natives waited for the appropriate moment, remembered the directions that had been given to them, rushed to the location, found the man sleeping and thrust their spears into the red blanket. Then they unwound the blanket to sever the head and found their Chinese friend, mortally wounded. He had given his life for his cause. That incident ended head-hunting on that Pacific island.

Jesus said, "Greater love hath no man than this, that a man lay down his life for his friends." Whenever we offer a day or a week of our lives to help another, whenever we live or die in a cause that is God's and man's, we live and die significantly, for this is sacrificial living, and sacrifice lies at the heart of the universe.

3

A Holy Kind of Carelessness

Carelessness is a "loaded" word. To most men's minds it means mischievous negligence or foolhardy thoughtlessness. Of course, such kinds of carelessness do abound, and they are ruinous. Nearly every week we read in our newspapers of someone who has "accidentally" killed himself playing Russian roulette. On a dare he placed a bullet in the chamber of a revolver. He spun the revolver cylinder so that he could not know whether the bullet-filled chamber or an empty one was in place when he put the muzzle to his head and pulled the trigger. What a stupid, wasteful way to die! This is an evil kind of carelessness.

Some carelessness is less dangerous but still show-offish. In the 1930's an official ban was posted against death-defying stunts attempted at Niagara Falls. Before the ban became effective, at least thirty-one persons engaged in some spectacular, daredevil feat designed more to attract attention than to prove any worthwhile purpose.

Nearly one-fourth of these people were killed either trying to swim through the thundering rapids or passing over the brink in a boat, in a barrel, or a rubber ball. This kind of carelessness cares less for safety than it does for display and applause. It is an unholy thing.

People who are indifferent to the physical pain and mental torture, the poverty and injustice, the ignorance and cruelty, war, hunger, and pestilence present in the world are careless in the most repugnant ways.

But there is a kind of carelessness that is neither self-consciously exhibitionistic nor diabolically thoughtless of another's welfare. It is wholesome and holy. The Psalmist possessed it and wrote, "I will fear no evil: for thou art with me." The Psalmist was *literally careless* — caring less than others did about life's dangers because he cared more about God's presence with him. He could take life's risks. He needed no guarantees of safety from disappointment, disaster, or death. All dangers could be endured if his spiritual resources were great enough. An awareness of God's nearness and love diminished concern for his own welfare. "Yea, though I walk through the valley of the shadow of death, I will fear no evil: for thou art with me." That is a holy kind of carelessness.

Carelessness about "what people will think" is a sacred virtue, enabling a person to act from pure conviction and a clear and uncluttered conscience. A conscience which yields to the fear of what "they" will think or say is always timid, always shaky, and never dependable. Pilate planned to act mercifully toward Jesus until he considered what the crowd might think.

When rightly used, carelessness concerning consequences can be a holy thing. When Socrates was on trial for his life he could have saved himself by a slight compromise with the demands of his persecutors. But he declared to his judges, "A man who is good for anything

SOCRATES

ought not to calculate the chances of living or dying; he ought to consider whether he is right or wrong." Such carelessness makes the exercise of other virtues possible. If we care too much about the predicaments virtues may get us into we may not develop them or practice them. The politician who will be honest only when honesty will lose him no votes is already tainted with dishonesty. The businessman who is truthful excepting when the truth costs him profits has a blemished sincerity. An honesty which is conditioned upon consequences is a shabby and undependable ethic. A patriotism that is conditioned upon taking no risks is untrustworthy. But when a virtue scorns consequences it demonstrates its real worth.

The answer to unwholesome fear is a wholehearted trust in God's concern, care, and provision for us — faith in the All-Sufficiency that surrounds our daily need. This does not mean that "everything will turn out all right" or as we wish. Rather, it means freedom from the anxiety that life's pressures may prove too burdensome for us or that the valley of the shadow may be too dark and lonely. Such trust even includes freedom from the fear of being afraid. "I will fear no evil, for thou art with me."

Holy carelessness means to care less about what life might do to us because we have come to care more for what God means to us.

4

We See What We Are Prepared to See

A Swiss mountain guide once warned a group of mountain climbers who were ascending the Jungfrau to keep their attention on the heights they were attempting to attain. He cautioned them that huge chunks of snow and ice sometimes break off the mountains at great distances from the climbers, but in the clear, crisp air of the heights the avalanches sound as if they are near, and novice climbers turn to look. Disaster often follows. They miss their step and fall in the direction of their attention, or they lean over too far to look, lose their balance and topple into the abyss. No matter what inviting distractions bid for attention, keep your eyes on your goal. So say the seasoned mountain guides. If we want to climb to the peaks, we must keep our attention fixed on the peaks, because *we tend to get what we are looking for.*

The mountain guide's warning is a good one to keep in mind at the beginning of a new year. Here we are in January. The year-end holidays are gone. Christmas is past, and with its passage there is danger that the values Christmas stands for may quickly be forgotten. Christmas trees have been taken down and the lights have been boxed and set away in the attic or basement. Gay wrappings have been smoothed out and stored or thrown into the trash burner. And what about Christmas reverence, Christmas wonder, Christmas delight in giving gifts and bringing joy to others? Do we put them in storage until next December?

Just when we are tempted to take our attention off the good things of which Christmas makes us aware, January 6th comes along. Throughout much of Christendom January 6th will bring Christmas truths into focus again,

for January 6th is celebrated in many churches as Epiphany. The word "Epiphany" has ancient origins, and comes from the Greek word meaning "to show" or "to make an appearance." Epiphany is the feast day commemorating the coming of the Wise Men to Bethlehem, when Christ was first "shown" to them. Supposedly they were the first Gentiles to see Him. (This day is sometimes called "Twelfth-night," because it follows Christmas by twelve nights.)

The Wise Men were seers, astrologers, the ancient forerunners of the astronomers. They were searchers of the skies for signs of what God was about to do with His world and with His people. And when the star that signaled Christ's coming appeared in the heavens, the Magi saw it and visited the Holy Child, bringing Him gifts.

The Wise Men saw what they were prepared to

see. They were looking for a Deliverer and for some sign, some star of hope, to guide them through the world's darkness and into His presence. Had they not been so earnest and eager in scanning the signs of the times and in watching the skies, the Wise Men might have missed Christ's coming. But they were prepared to see the star and ready to see the Saviour.

But if the star was there for Wise Men to behold, was it not there for all to see? It was there for the throngs who visited Bethlehem and crowded the inn, but who did not know of the glory that passed them by. It hung there in the night sky for the busy innkeeper, for the soldiers who marched down the cobblestone streets. But, if they saw it at all, they missed its meaning. The Wise Men saw the star and followed it to where the Holy Child lay because the Wise Men were *looking* for the star.

Isn't this the way it is with life: we see what we are prepared to see? The scientist seeks greater knowledge, and is mentally ready to find it. He is open-minded and humble enough to know that he knows very little. The scientist believes that if he takes the right steps, follows the right principles, is thoughtful and imaginative enough, he may discover new truth. The scientist who finds more light shed upon dark mystery sees the light because he is inwardly prepared to see it.

Wise men of every age are those who are searching for some sign from God, and they see what they are looking for. When they attend worship, they enter the sanctuary with a reverent, receptive, hopeful attitude toward God. Those who attend church seeking anything less than God will find that, too! If it is respectability or sociability they are looking for, they will find it. If it is fault with the church, its minister or its members, they will find that. It is said that a member of his congregation greeted Henry Ward Beecher at the church door after a worship service with the news, "Dr. Beecher, you may be interested to know that I counted a dozen grammatical errors in your sermon this morning." And the noted preacher responded, "I wouldn't be much surprised if I made two dozen such errors." But another worshipper left the same church that morning saying, "Today I found God." Both men found what they were prepared to find.

Wise men now, as of old, are still looking for some sign of God. They search for the good in their churches, in the world at large, in their immediate communities, in each other. This does not mean that the wise ignore the evil in the world. As Saint Matthew's Gospel tells us, the Magi became acquainted with evil Herod as well as with the infant Jesus. But it was not Herod that they searched for, nor was he their chief interest. Herod was not the one for whom they brought gifts. They did not rejoice over Herod or worship him. They were prepared to see a star and the Saviour. They found what they were looking for. We usually do.

5

Some Said It Thundered

We live in a world where appearances are deceptive, where the extraordinary often looks like everyday stuff.

The Gospel of John tells of an event in the life of Jesus close to the end of His earthly ministry: He had dined with His friends and He then went to Jerusalem where a great crowd gathered to see Him. There followed a clamorous public demonstration of acclaim. Nearly the entire city turned out for the occasion, some out of curiosity and others in admiration edging on worship. But Jesus seemed somewhat aloof from it all. He sensed that His death was near. Perhaps it would come at the hands of some of those who now watched Him ride through the streets. He trusted that good would come from His dying, and He prayed, "Father, glorify thy name." "Then," says the Gospel, "a voice came from heaven, 'I have glorified it, and I will glorify it again.' The crowd standing by heard it and said that it had thundered. Others said, 'An angel has spoken to him.' "

This was a crowd in which everyone heard the same sound. But how variously the people interpreted the sound! The Gospel writer informs us that the sound was from heaven and bore a message of reassurance to Jesus. A few thought an angel had spoken. But most members of the throng standing near the Master lightly shrugged the matter off, saying, "It's thundering."

This passage of Scripture reminds us of something vital about human nature wherever we find it — in ancient Jerusalem or in our town today: we are not so much affected by what happens to us as we are by our interpretation of what happens. We can be like the Jerusalem crowd in the presence of greatness and miss it, or we can be caught up in an earth-shaking event and be quite unaffected by it all. We sometimes shrug off the highest things we see because they seem so commonplace. We look at what others see and hear what others hear, but we miss the grandeur and the meaning.

Most advancements in science are based upon someone's noticing what others missed, upon someone's reverent regard for the high revelation that lurks behind life's drab commonplaceness. For centuries men watched lightning streak across the sky, and they casually said, "It will soon rain. I saw lightning." But their sight was not blessed with insight, and they beheld nothing in lightning but light and the possibility of disaster to anything the lightning might strike.

Then Benjamin Franklin began to wonder if there was not more than meets the eye in lightning. Suppose that our eyes missed something significant. In 1752 Franklin experimented with a silk kite, a piece of silk ribbon, a long string, a piece of wire, and a key fastened to the kite string, and raised the kite in a thunderstorm. Franklin got sparks from the key tied to the rain-soaked kite string. This was one of the earliest investigations into the nature of electricity and how it is conducted, and all the world has profited from the refusal of one man to shrug his shoulders at a flash of light in the sky and mutter, "It is only lightning."

Franklin knew that all commonplace things will give up meaning to the alert and sensitive person as certainly as mountains surrender precious ores to those who look beneath the surface.

Our nation's greatness can be largely credited to men of courageous insight who looked with hope upon events that shocked others with utter despair. In January of 1778 George Washington wrote from Valley Forge to the President of the Continental Congress, reporting that only five hundred and seventy-two of his troops were capable of duty. "Unless there is a great and capital change, this army must inevitably be reduced to one or other of these three things: starve, dissolve, or disperse in order to obtain subsistence in the best manner they can." Almost three thousand of Washington's men were unfit for duty because of near nakedness. Many were barefooted. Some men deserted; their interpretation of

events was that the war was unendurable and quite hopeless. Washington stayed through discouraging, heart-
breaking days, suffered the woes of his soldiers, and interpreted the conflict as worthy of pursuit. All saw the
same facts. How differently they interpreted them!

In pity at man's dullness and insensibility to God's activity, Hans Denk once exclaimed, "O my God, how does
it happen in this poor old world that Thou art so great
and nobody finds Thee, that Thou callest so loudly and
nobody hears Thee, that Thou art so near and nobody
feels Thee, that Thou givest Thyself to everybody and
nobody knows Thy name? Men flee from Thee and
say they cannot see Thee; they stop their ears and say
they cannot hear Thee."

Could we miss hearing God's voice amidst the clashing
noises of international strife in our time? Perhaps. Is
it possible that what we have interpreted to be a meaningless uproar of unpleasant world events is the judgment of
Heaven saying something significant to the children of
earth, telling us that we no longer have a choice, as we
once did, between justice and injustice? The choice
now is between justice among men and death. We cannot choose now between international understanding and
forgiveness on the one hand and war on the other. The
option is between understanding and good will or an-
nihilation. That sound we hear, is it earth's thunder or is
it God having His say?

And how about your personal, daily life? If your
situation seems drab and undramatic, do not blame your
circumstance for your impoverishment of spiritual riches.
Accuse yourself. Tell yourself that you are not aware
of God because you are looking for lesser things. Explain
to yourself that you do not hear His voice because earth's
lesser sounds are too important to you, or because when
God speaks you misinterpret the voice to be "only duty

calling" or "just a twinge of conscience" or "a mere impulse" to perform a kindness.

God still speaks, and to all of us.

He still searches for those who will hear and recognize and obey His voice.

6

Trifles Make Tremendous Differences

Pliny the Elder, a contemporary of Saint Paul, said of the Romans of his day that when they failed to make a thing beautiful they were sure to make it big. Apparently even Jesus' disciples were caught up in the Roman fascination for bigness. One time as the Master and His disciples left the temple, a disciple exclaimed, "Look, Teacher, what wonderful stones and what wonderful buildings!" One 'translator catches the spirit of the awed one when he has him saying, "What a size these stones and buildings are!" Jesus did not frown upon the magnificence of the temple buildings. Doubtlessly He rejoiced in such grandeur. But while the disciples were enamored of sheer bigness, something else caught Jesus' attention — a little thing: a poor woman putting two copper coins in the temple treasury, demonstrating sacrificial dedication to a holy cause. Jesus noticed this, and it impressed Him. To Jesus' mind a sacrifice of two copper coins, when it represented everything a woman owned, was far more notable than a huge stone or a big building.

In Christ's scale of values little things had tremendous worth. When He spoke of a final judgment He told of *little* people doing *little* things in loving ways receiving the blessing of the King. However, when the blessed ones were feeding the hungry, or giving drink to the thirsty, or lodging to the stranger, or clothing to the naked, or solace and companionship to the sick and imprisoned, they did not know these ministries were great in Christ's eye. Love, rather than hope of reward, impelled them. And they did not realize that Christ had any connection with the needs of the people they served. When Christ identified Himself as one who was fed when the hungry were served and as one who was comforted when the sick and imprisoned were called upon, the righteous exclaimed, "Lord, when did we see *thee*. . . ?" and He answered ". . . As you did it unto one of the least of these my brethren, you did it to me." So even the blessed ones missed the importance of doing little things for the world's little people. They did not see that little things and little people are great in Christ's eyes.

In a world that worships bigness we need to accept Christ's standard of values. Especially do we need to develop and use His high regard for the importance of little things. James Russell Lowell had "the mind of Christ" at this point. James Thomas Fields, the American author and publisher, once received this advice from Lowell: "Be sure and don't leave anything out because it is trifling; for it is out of trifles only that it is possible to reconstruct character, sometimes, if not always."

Tiny trifles have enormous influences. They can frustrate or fulfill us. The things that cause us the most irritation are seldom life's catastrophic problems. Just as a litle dirt in a fuel line of an automobile can stop the car

LOWELL

as effectively as a broken axle, so can a little defect in a life make for as much misery as a major fault. A jumping nerve in a tooth can momentarily push a person to the brink of madness; yet the nerve is a tiny thing. A mosquito can drive a strong man to distraction more quickly than a swarm of military planes maneuvering over his head. Someone has wisely prayed, "O Lord, deliver us from the gnats. We can take care of the elephants ourselves." Men who have been at their best under extreme testing have fallen apart under life's petty annoyances. One American flier who won the plaudits of the Western world for bravery during World War II has gone from job to job, from marriage to marriage, and from bad to worse since that war ended. He had enough character for life's great emergencies but not enough to face everyday problems.

Repeatedly people request help from counselors in straightening out a desperate domestic tangle, and when they are asked what the big problem might be they reply, "There is no big problem; but a lot of little ones make our marriage unbearable." The husband provides well for the family. The wife cooks and keeps house in expert fashion. Neither has ever threatened to shoot the other or shown a great meanness. But little by little petty annoyances have revealed hidden impatience and peevishness or provoked anger and exasperation, and a relationship that could have withstood the earthquake of a sudden disappointment of disastrous proportions is destroyed by the slow erosion of little irritants.

But, thank Heaven, small things work for our triumph as well as for our ruin. An ancient Chinese proverb reminds us, "The man who removed the mountain was he who began carrying away the small stones." Often "faith removes mountains" in just that way. The greatest tasks are accomplished little by little, and all who have learned to do big things well have begun by learning to do little things faithfully.

The longest walk is taken with single steps.

The man who learns to put his moments to good use need not worry about the outcome of his days or of his life.

The beauties of the visible world greet our minds after traveling over a tiny, fragile pathway, the optic nerve.

The vast universe is composed of submicroscopic atoms, revealing the Creator's regard for the smallest things.

Well, how about our consciousness of values? Does it take notice of little things like coins and cups of water and brief visits to the needy? Is it becoming more like that of Christ, with a great respect for little things handled in loving ways?

7

Do You Know What You're Doing?

Every deed we perform is far greater in its consequences than our wildest guesses can imagine. We never can know the long-range effects of our simplest actions. Nothing we do is as trivial as it seems to be.

The future of Christianity once perilously hung by a rope made by an unknown craftsman who never guessed the momentous consequences of making a *good* rope. Shortly after his conversion, Paul, the Apostle to the Gentiles, was watched closely by his enemies while he visited in Damascus. They plotted to capture him as he passed through the city's gates. But, as the author of the Acts of the Apostles puts it, "His disciples took him by night and let him down over the wall, lowering him in a basket." The Damascus wall was high. Men attached ropes to a large basket and lowered Paul from the top of the wall to the ground, safe outside the city. All Christendom is the beneficiary of Paul's courageous evangelism. More than any other of Christ's followers, Paul transformed the early Christian fellowship from a sect within the Jewish religion into a world faith. Yet, if Christianity owes gratitude to Paul, we must not forget, either, those un-named disciples who made his ministry possible, in the deep of the night letting him down over the high Damas-cus wall in a basket, and some unmentioned basket-maker who made a durable basket that did not pull apart under Paul's weight. And it is a peculiarity of my faith that when I think thankfully of what Christianity means to the world, and how Gentile Christianity can be traced largely to the labors and genius of Paul, I often breathe a prayer of praise for some unnamed, unknown rope-maker who, when he made ropes, made *good* ropes.

Suppose the rope that held Paul in his basket had been made of old or unseasoned materials, so that under the strain of the Apostle's weight it had snapped. Had Paul fallen from that high wall, had Paul been killed, what a different world this might be. But the rope did not break. Paul did not fall. Someone had made a *good* rope.

The unknown rope-maker illustrates what it means to live a life of trust. Trusting means to have the assurance that God has an interest in our work, and when we have done our best we can be certain He will prosper the re-sults in ways that exceed our fondest hopes. Life's conse-quences are in better hands than our own. Every crafts-man needs to know that. Every honest, dedicated states-man should remember that. Especially all fretful, anxiety-ridden parents should keep it in mind. There is a Power in the universe that takes our faithfulness to the best we know and works wonders with it. Long after tears have been wiped from two-year-old cheeks and years after bruised four-year-old knees have been bandaged and healed, long after adolescent struggles for independence have quieted and graduation ceremonies have been at-tended and youthful marriage vows spoken — long after you have done your tender, loving, level best, God continues working in his Results Department prospering every good deed you thought to be so trivial, or meaningless, or futile.

This is a universe in which an unknown craftsman can make a rope, the best rope he knows how to make, and then let it go out into the world, unwittingly helping to make Christ's gospel available to us nearly two thou-

sand years after the rope left his little workshop. We can trust the Power that brings such great consequences out of simple faithfulness to high standards.

The secret of life is knowing how to let go, once we have put our finished tasks and best deeds into God's hands.

8

Needed: Some Maladjusted Men!

At his best, man is the maladjusted creature, chronically dissatisfied with things as they are. Because man had difficulty adjusting himself to cold air and cold food he invented the home fire for warmth and cooking. Because he was discontented with his legs as means of locomotion man invented the boat and the wheel and domesticated horses for riding purposes. Fretting over inadequate means of communication, man invented complex languages to express his thought and feeling and went on to create writing, printing, the telephone, telegraph, radio and television. No other animals have done these things. None have felt a need for better things; they have been adjusted to things as they are.

We humans are adjusted to maladjustment. When life is somewhat difficult for us and we are "out of kilter" with our environment, we often prosper from the strain. When life is too easy for us, we suffer from excess comfort. Have you ever been sentenced to several weeks of bed rest? One would guess that such prolonged repose would strengthen a patient. However, while quietness and inactivity may be curative as far as the affliction is concerned, extended physical idleness raises problems of its own. It weakens the muscles until any mild exercise is exhausting. Muscles require opposition and struggle to keep their tone.

One would think that walking over smooth, hard pavement would be much easier than tramping over rough meadows, rolling hills or forest trails. City sidewalks and pavements were built especially for man's convenience, to make locomotion more comfortable. Nevertheless, few tasks are more tiring than a day's walk on concrete that has been laid for man's convenience. Concrete pavings are especially fitted to man, and supposedly man is adjusted to pavements. But his body responds better to rough ground, to the harsher environment of the natural world. Too much adjustment is hard on man.

We need more and better maladjustments in human society. In the realms of morals and spirit, adjustment to things as they are is crippling to character, and it stifles progress. The welfare of humankind depends upon the courage of some members of society to be different from the rest. They must go beyond the easy, comfortable morality of those around them. They are better than the law requires and better than man expects them to be, although being different will surely cause them trouble.

In the fifth chapter of the Acts of the Apostles we learn of the ecclesiastical trial of Peter and John. This occurred in the early days of the Christian era when Christianity had a youthful vitality and when it was dangerous to be a Christian. Then, as now, it was desirable to be in adjustment to one's social environment, to agree with the authorities, to merge one's own principles and practices with those of the secular world, to "blend in." "When

PETER

JOHN

COPERNICUS

in Rome, do as the Romans do" was safe advice, for in those times the penalty for nonconformity was severe — frequently jail and sometimes death. Peter and John were wholeheartedly committed to Christ and the Christian cause, and they had long since discovered that dedication to the will of God often means maladjustment to the will of man. Taken before an ecclesiastical council, they were charged with preaching a new, unorthodox and revolutionary gospel. At the trial they were forbidden to teach the Christian message. To this demand they answered, "We must obey God rather than men." This enraged members of the council who wanted to kill the apostles, but Gamaliel, a great, honored teacher of the law, dissuaded the troubled elders, and the apostles were released after a severe beating. They returned to their preaching, still dangerously maladjusted to the world as they found it.

The best servants of mankind have always been maladjusted to their times. They dared to be difficult, to think differently, to act differently. Christ did, and His apostles did, or there would be no Christianity. Copernicus and Galileo and others did, or we would still believe in a pygmy universe. Inventors did, or we would still be plowing fields with a stick and lighting our houses with torches or candles. The Abolitionists and Abraham Lincoln did, or we would still have slavery. Robert E. Lee did, or the aftermath of the War Between the States would have ended with greater rancor and less forgiveness. Mankind's most noble servants have refused to become adjusted to man's cruelty to man, to predatory economic practices, to the idea that disease is inevitable and useless to oppose, to dictatorships, to the persecution of minorities, to race prejudice, to narrow nationalism, to the war method of solving international differences. For conscience's sake, for man's sake and for God's sake they lived daringly. They rejected the premium that others put on a safe conformity and they ventured to become uncommon men. They did not parrot the opinions of others but spoke their own clean, sharp words. They did not blend in, but stood out even when it was perilous to be "outstanding."

How about you? Do you tend to become conformed, blended with the masses, losing your God-given individuality?

Do you let advertisements dictate your tastes, adjusting your thinking and buying to what others are doing around you? Advertising pleads with us to become standardized, to be "in fashion," to wear what others are wearing, eat what others are eating, drink what others are drinking, drive what others are driving, read what others are reading. Do you give glad answers to these invitations to uniformity, to mass-mindedness, to a pathological escape from your own uniqueness?

Do you unthinkingly bow your knees to custom and tradition without examining their values?

Does "Everybody's doing it!" seem an adequate justification for almost any behavior? For common vulgarities? For heavy drinking? For laxity in matters of sex?

Do you have only impressions, opinions, and theories that change with the shifting winds of public opinion and practice, or do you hold mighty convictions that give you steadiness and strength when others waver?

Are you a voice or merely an echo?

Would you rather be wrong and approved by others, or right and ridiculed?

Some years ago a telephone operator in a small Cape Cod town received a daily call from a man who asked for the exact time. This went on for many weeks. Finally the operator asked the caller why he called every day requesting the correct time. The man replied, "I must get the exact time, because I am the man responsible for blowing the town whistle precisely at noon each day."

GALILEO

LINCOLN

LEE

49

"Well, that's mighty odd," the operator replied, "because every day, exactly at noon, I set my clock by your whistle."

A parable of life! We tend to get our time, our moral standards, our principles from one another. Being adjusted to each other we become maladjusted to God.

Like Peter and John, we need to get our time from the heavens.

9

Limatations Have Their Limits

All forms of life are encircled by limitations that they must struggle against. Most fish are so created that they can survive only in water, and if they are removed from water for even a few minutes, they die. Many trees, such as the redwoods of the Pacific Coast, have specific humidity and warmth requirements. They cannot grow anywhere where the moisture in the air or the temperature falls below a certain level, so they inhabit a small area where their conditions for growth are met and they are prevented from spreading by barriers of valleys, deserts and climates that are too dry, too cold or too hot.

Man's body temperature needs to fluctuate only a few degrees up or down the temperature scale and he dies. His cells must contain a certain minimum of moisture or he perishes of dehydration. A few grains less of thyroxin in his blood stream makes him an imbecile, and a little too much thyroxin makes him a physical and nervous wreck.

Nearly every living thing is surrounded with limitations. Yet fish, deprived of atmospheric breathing, make the most of their watery environment and become ingenious at maintaining a home in it. Coast redwoods, in spite of their limitations, grow to be among the biggest and oldest of living organisms. Man, with all his restrictions, is the creature that seems to crave still more of them and invents games that compel the players to struggle against contrived limitations.

Our best-loved American sports impinge restrictions upon the players. Baseball would lose much of its charm if every batter were given an unlimited number of chances to hit the ball. Three strikes is every player's limit. Football and basketball would lose much of their fascination if the games had no narrow time limits in which the teams must do all their scoring. And what enjoyment would tennis provide if nets and boundary lines were removed from the courts? The limitations imposed upon players are part of the game.

During a dense fog in London a man and his wife got off a subway, reached the exit, and discovered they could not find their way to their home, which was only a short distance away. While they studied how they might make their way through the thick, clammy whiteness, a stranger overheard their anxious discussion and asked if he might help them. They thanked him for his offer and asked how someone they did not know could find their way home when they themselves were made helpless by the fog. The stranger answered, "I'm blind." Then he explained that he lived in the neighborhood and because of his affliction had memorized the streets, the location of sidewalks, curbs, lampposts and houses. All day he had worked joyously, guiding people who were lost in the fog. The blind man's severe limitation had its own limits. He was kept from seeing, but he could not be barred from a happy usefulness.

Christianity is the beneficiary of one who knew that it is a man's abilities, not his disabilities, that count. He outwitted his handicaps. The Apostle Paul was harassed by a physical limitation that irritated him

LONDON FOG

considerably. He referred to it as his "thorn in the flesh" but did not otherwise identify it. We do know he was sick during a part of his ministry. Some scholars believe Paul's affliction was epilepsy, or possibly recurrent attacks of malaria, and some are convinced it was eye trouble. Paul said, "Three times I besought the Lord about this, that it should leave me; but he said to me, 'My grace is sufficient for you, for my power is made perfect in weakness.'" Whatever the nature of Paul's handicap, his limitation had limits! In spite of it Paul established Christian churches among the Gentiles and became Christianity's greatest missionary. He took his faith to Europe and rooted it there. While imprisoned for his faith he wrote letters which have become the inspiration of millions and the basis for an understanding of the Christian way of life.

Frustrating handicaps have been unable to curb the usefulness of many of the world's best-known people. While they were annoyed by their limitations, their purposes could not be thwarted by their afflictions. Julius Caesar was an epileptic. So was Dostoevski. Homer and John Milton were blind. John Keats and Robert Louis Stevenson suffered from tuberculosis. Alexander Pope and Charles Steinmetz were hunchbacks. Lord Nelson had one eye. Ludwig van Beethoven and Thomas Edison were deaf. Lord Byron was clubfooted, and Edgar Allan Poe a psychoneurotic. Moses stammered. Somerset Maugham tells us that his habit of stammering prompted him to become a writer. Glen Cunningham, one of the great "milers" of all time, was so badly burned in the legs as a child that it was thought he would never walk again. Louis Pasteur did much of his work upon which modern medicine rests after suffering a paralytic stroke. And Franklin Roosevelt's years of public service came largely after he was stricken with infantile paralysis. George Washington's home, Mount Vernon, was preserved as a national shrine through the efforts of Pamela Cunningham, an invalid with a spinal affliction who wrote letters from her sickroom and raised money to purchase Mt. Vernon, even when her illness was so debilitating that she sometimes went into convulsions from the exertion of signing her name. Helen Keller used her deafness and blindness to shut out the world's distractions, enabling her to concentrate on life's meaning. She thus became one of the most reflective and profound people of her generation.

Some of these men and women rose to eminence because of the stimulus of their physical defects. Their capacities found incentive for growth in their apparently hostile limitations.

What is the secret of handling our disturbing limitations? The best we can do is to regard the capacities we have left as God's gracious gifts to us, to be developed and to be used for purposes that have His approval and that will serve human need.

A young Italian shows us how. He lost both eyes and an arm while working in an American stone quarry. His fellow workers were careless in handling dynamite, and the Italian youth paid for their negligence with pain and loss. A woman who had lived in Italy for a brief while and learned to speak Italian frequently called upon the young Italian in the hospital, cheered him and gave him hope, and when he was well enough arranged for his admission to a school for the blind. The lad proved to be an able, avid scholar with a receptive mind and a sharp intellect. Several years after he entered the institution to study he became the most popular teacher in that school. He happily attributed his success to what at first had been a tragedy, declaring, "The day of my accident was the birthday of my mind."

Every limitation has its limits. When life imposes a handicap upon us, the restriction opens new opportunities. The end of one possibility is the beginning of another. This is God's way.

10

Don't Just Stand There. Do Something!

Each year we celebrate Columbus Day on October 12th, for it was on that day in 1492 that Christopher Columbus discovered America. Other men before Columbus believed that the world must be round rather than flat and that the East might be reached by sailing westward. But Columbus was the first man known to act upon his belief. It is his action that we celebrate on Columbus Day and not his theory. The world always commemorates deeds rather than theories, for we intuitively know that all the idealistic beliefs heaped together are worth less than one courageous deed.

The Bible warns against the substitutes we so easily make for good deeds. Good words, for instance. Pretty words, charitable words make convenient replacements for action. It is always easier to "talk a good line" than it is to live a good life. The First Epistle of John warns, "Little children, let us not love in word or speech but in deed. . . ." Splendid deeds, rather than sweet words, make for real eloquence.

Like lovely words, soft sentimentalism easily becomes a substitute for shining deeds. We assume we have done something significant for people when we have merely felt sorry for them. C. S. Lewis, in his *Screwtape Letters*, pictures an old, experienced devil advising a young devil that he must let folks feel pity for others. That will give them a glow of good feeling. But stop people from expressing good feeling in good deeds, and soon they won't even entertain good feelings, so the crafty old devil advised. And it's devilishly true.

George Eliot, whose real name was Marian Evans Cross, was one of the most distinguished of English women novelists. She felt deeply about human misery and wrote about it, but she did nearly nothing to relieve the tragedy she saw around her. She said her faith in God diminished when she saw the world so full of heartache and hopelessness. George Eliot did little about it besides sitting at her desk and speculating on why evil should be allowed in the world. George MacDonald, the Scottish poet, novelist and clergyman, lived in George Eliot's day. He suffered more misery than George Eliot ever saw. Plagued by serious illnesses, at one time MacDonald could not speak or write for a period of three years. His son died. His parishioners boycotted him and would not pay his salary because his preaching was too simple and too direct for their taste. But he spent his days in compassionate helpfulness wherever he saw human need. George MacDonald declared, "Nothing makes one feel so strong as a call for help." MacDonald heard the calls. He answered.

In every community there are the George Eliots who see need, wax sentimental about it, and lament, "Why is it permitted? Why doesn't somebody do something about it?" And nearly everywhere, thank Heaven, there is some George MacDonaldlike soul who senses the same need and feels the same sentiment, and does something about it.

Good deeds have another advantage over good feelings. Besides being more effectual in helping the world, our deeds can be controlled better than our emotions. There is hope here for those of us who regret our uncharitable feelings toward our neighbors. If our affections are less than we wish them to be, our deeds can be better than our emotions. Our feelings will not always comply with our commands, but our feet and hands and faces are more likely to follow orders. I cannot decide, "At 6:15 this evening I shall begin loving my neighbor as myself," and be certain that my emotions will obey my order. But at 6:15 my feet will obey my command to walk to my neighbor's house. My hand will do my bidding and knock at my neighbor's door. My lips will carry out my orders and form the words, "Hello, Charles! For some time I've been wanting to offer my help. . . ." And, soon or late, better feelings will follow in the wake of better behavior, if the behavior is persistent. Repeated kindly deeds will make for kindliness. Cheerful acts can lead to cheerfulness. "Love your enemies, do good to them which hate you," Jesus said. Love is the goal. Doing good is the way to reach it. By doing our neighbors good we come to love them.

When anyone puts a limit on what he will do, he thereby limits what he can feel and what he can be. Act the way you would like to be and you will soon be the way you act.

By converting a belief into a deed, Christopher Columbus discovered a new world. By expressing our best thoughts and highest principles in helpful actions we can find a new life.

11

What Gets Your Attention?

What gets your attention? Does the evil in the world attract you, or does the good? Do you give more heed to life's difficulties or to its joys? Are you more attentive to your neighbor's faults or to his virtues? Do you mourn the days and the years that have passed or rejoice in this day which is yours? Do you give more notice to all that you possess or to all that you lack?

Whatever gets our attention and holds it witnesses to what we are. Whether we are dull and dimsighted spirits or vitally alive will be shown by what we notice, what we are most mindful of and what absorbs our attention.

There are two words that have a special meaning as Thanksgiving Day approaches. Both words are related to this matter of our attentiveness. One is the word "cynical" which comes from the ancient Greek word meaning "doglike." Cynics in the ancient world were violent critics of social customs and philosophies. They tended to be pessimistic about all men, believing human conduct was mostly motivated by selfishness. Presumably they were described by the Greeks as doglike because they wore a downward "hang-dog," beaten, tail-between-the-legs look. Because cynics looked downward, what they saw in life was the dirt beneath their feet. No wonder they thought all the world was dirty.

The other meaningful word is "anthropoid," meaning "manlike." The anthropoid apes are the manlike creatures that walk like men, on their hind legs. "Anthropology" is a related word. Coming from the same root, *anthropos,* it means the study of man, his physique, distribution, social relationships, customs. The root word *anthropos* means "man" when loosely translated into English, but more literally it means "the creature that looks up." At his best, man is such a creature — upward-looking.

While there is no possibility of saying with certainty what animals think about, so far as we can discover, man is the only creature that aspires to be better than he is. He is the only one that worships the Unseen and asks for help in becoming what he should be. Man is the only creature that ever observes a Thanksgiving Day. Other animals live through perilous winters, exist on scanty rations, nearly starve, sicken and almost die as did the Puritans of Plymouth Colony who later celebrated the First Thanksgiving. But the surviving animals remain literally cynical, doglike, downward-looking. Only man is capable of looking up in wonder, awe and gratitude.

I have often watched pigs feeding on fallen apples in an old orchard. They gorged themselves on the succulent fruit without ever looking up to see where the apples came from. This is the cynical view of life, the doglike, hoglike, downward look.

But when man is most truly man, he gives thanks. He looks up to the Source of all good things. When the Sioux Indians of the Dakotas killed buffalo and enjoyed a great feast, an Indian woman would cut a piece of buffalo steak and deliberately drop it into the fire. It was a religious sacrament. She praised the Creator for provisions for Indian needs and asked a blessing upon the food, saying, "Great Spirit, we thank Thee for the plentiful gifts Thou hast given us, and we ask Thee to partake with us."

In like fashion the Puritans were doing the "manly," human thing, the thing that fits human nature, when, after the fruits of the earth were gathered in and the fall hunt was over, they set aside a time for uplifting grateful hearts in prayer and praise. Of course, they, too, like subhuman creatures of the Plymouth fields and forests, had to look down sometimes, especially if they were to plant, cultivate and harvest food from the generous earth. But they were aware that there would be no seed to plant, no crops, no harvest, no turkey or deer to roast, if it were not for the Divine Care above and behind all living things. So they looked upward in glad thanksgiving. And they spread this attitude from Thanksgiving Day over all their days until they were able to say with the Psalmist, "Every

day will I bless thee; and I will praise thy name for ever and ever" (Psalm 145:2).

How about us? Are we cynics or upward-looking people of faith?

The cynic looks down upon all that he has as unsatisfactory. It is not enough. He is absorbed in what he still lacks. One of Andrew Carnegie's relatives was greatly provoked at Andrew when the rich old philanthropist died and left the relative a million dollars. It was not enough. Carnegie had offended him by giving 365 million dollars to charity and cutting him off with "one measly million."

The person of faith looks upon what he has and is grateful for it. One woman bore several children, although she and her husband could ill afford a large family. She nurtured them and sent them into the world as disciplined, responsible, well-trained servants of mankind. She had always found time, too, for neighborly deeds of kindness. After years of unselfish labor, cooking, washing, ironing, cleaning, she suffered a severe stroke. For days her life precariously hung by a thread of vitality. Then she began to gain strength, although she remained in bed for weeks. After a time she could sit for a while in a chair. There a visitor found her by the fire. She greeted him with a smile and an exclamation, "Am I not the lucky one? Look, I've got the use of my right hand!" She belonged to the society of the grateful ones, the people of the upward look.

At Thanksgiving time one little girl was asked to tell what she was most grateful for, and she thought hard and long. Then she said, "I am thankful that I am thankful."

It may be that of all the blessings we have received, a grateful heart, the impulse toward the upward look, is the best of all.

12

From Grumbling to Gratitude

The common conception of Thanksgiving Day is that it originated as a festival of praise to God for the abundance of good things the Almighty had bestowed upon the Pilgrim Fathers at Plymouth Colony. Quite to the contrary, there was no such abundance. The Pilgrims seemingly had little for which they could be thankful.

Their first winter on the inhospitable shores of the new land was hard on them. Housing was inadequate, and the winds and cold were unmerciful. Approximately one-half of the members of the colony died in the first few months after the Pilgrims' arrival in North America. These settlers had established a small trading post, hoping to barter with friendly Indians. But a plague broke out among the Indians and many red men succumbed to the disease. The trading post then failed. The Pilgrims' small fishing industry was unsuccessful. A share-the-work program, that also permitted sharing the food,

PLYMOUTH COLONY

was a miserable failure, wrecked by self-interests and petty jealousies. When the first harvest time arrived the Pilgrims had eleven crude buildings, a twenty-acre crop of corn, a meager wheat harvest, very little barley, and peas that were not worth harvesting.

One would think that, far from feeling grateful to God, the Pilgrims might more logically have assembled for registering their complaints and sharing their woes. They had fled the Old World so that they might find freedom to worship God as led by conscience and by their highest insights. But what did their faithfulness get them? Disappointment, hardship, sickness, death, grief, and other miseries were their rewards. Grumbling seemed more appropriate than gratitude. Nevertheless, the Pilgrims assembled with a few Indian friends to thank God for what they had left after disaster had done its worst. When they reviewed the past they remembered that they were free from the religious persecution they had suffered in England. A few friendly Indians remained near Plymouth, especially the wise, goodhearted Squanto. He was their guide to understanding the secrets of wilderness living, and he advised them in agriculture. And the Pilgrims believed that enough heroic, hardship-seasoned pioneers survived to sustain a colony of freedom and piety on the northeast coast of the new land. For these blessings that were still theirs, after adversity had done its utmost to destroy them, the Pilgrims gave thanks.

The real point of Thanksgiving Day, then, is that we should be grateful when life is preserved and sustained, and not wait for some occasion of overwhelming good fortune before we thank God. When life is liberal with blessings, when Nature's bounty overflows fields, granaries and storehouses, it is hardly a Pilgrim virtue to praise God. Even the chronic grouch might manage to cast an appreciative thought upward then. But the Pilgrim Fathers considered *merely enough* a great plenty. In token of this attitude, for many years after the first Thanksgiving, Pilgrim parents placed five grains of corn upon each dinner plate before the Thanksgiving Day meal. When their children asked the meaning of the five kernels of corn the parents explained that at one time food was so scarce in Plymouth Colony that each person was given an allowance of five grains of corn each day to keep him alive. Still they were grateful to be alive, and gave thanks. And that first Thanksgiving festival was but the consummation of gratitude they had expressed all along through days of scarcity. They could easily give thanks in November because they had practiced it so faithfully all year.

The Plymouth Pilgrims' attitude of thanksgiving points to two basic clues to better living. First, we must choose the attitude with which we shall face life. Will it be with grumbling or with gratitude? An old law of physics states that Nature abhors a vacuum. So does human nature. The mind must be filled up, and if it is not loaded with appreciations it is likely to be heaped with complaints. The Pilgrims seemed to sense this. They had plenty to complain about, but who wants a mind burdened with moans and groans, with whimperings and mutterings? Tracing their steps over the past hard months, their memories picked up every blessing that could be found, and they came to Thanksgiving with minds spilling over with an abundance of appreciation. They had no room for complaints. Thus the Pilgrims taught us a prime secret of being grateful: everyone must choose from his experience what he will be most attentive to, life's adversities or its blessings. Gratitude is less a matter of what happens to us than it is a matter of choosing which of the things that happen to us we will dwell upon, and with what kind of attitude. Gratitude is discretion. It is man's power of choice exalted to its highest function.

Secondly, the aftermath of the first Thanksgiving was more work to improve Plymouth Colony. After thanks were said for life and food, for freedom and friends; after the food disappeared and the dishes were done, the Pilgrims returned to the drudgery of enlarging the clearing in the forest and pushing back the wilderness. Now, as then, the appreciators are the best workers. Not everything is right with America. But the people who are trying to set America right are not the chronic complainers. They are the grateful ones. They see our nation's faults, but they also glory in its goodness, and they set to work to make a good country better by the daily practice of responsible citizenship.

Every human society has its weaknesses, as did the colony at Plymouth. Every nation, every church, every club, every family has its faults. But the benefactors are those who, while seeing the faults, are grateful for the good they behold. They thank God and work for improvement. They know they can't remove the dents from a bucket by pounding it from the outside. One must see the bucket still has worth and then get inside it to fix it. The Pilgrim attitude is gratitude for the good and involvement in improving the imperfect.

In the One Hundreth Psalm the ancient writer sang, "Serve the Lord with gladness." Gladness and service are twin attitudes always. In Plymouth days they belonged together. They go together now.

13

What Do You Have to Offer?

In certain early American Indian tribes, when a princess came of age she was given a basket and instructed to pick the best ears of corn in a given row. There was one condition she must abide by: she must choose the ears as she went along. She could not turn back, retrace her steps, and select ears she had passed by. Many a princess failed this test of judgment. She marveled at the high quality of the corn, and as she felt of the firm ears on the stalks she was tempted to pick them. But perhaps there were better ears on the stalks just ahead. She would wait and see. Then suddenly, to her surprise and bitter disappointment, she found herself at the end of the corn row, and her basket was empty. While looking for perfection, she missed gathering any ears at all.

Life is like that. We move through our days constantly looking for the golden opportunity, the big chance, the lucky break, the perfect situation. We wish to improve our minds, enlighten and sharpen them, but perhaps

PUEBLO CORN — A BUSHY, LOW-GROWING GRAIN

there will be a better opportunity later on. We have the best intentions of becoming better people. We will go to church, become dedicated children of God, give time and money to Christ's cause, but all of this must come later, when the children are grown, when our job is more secure, or when our spouse develops the same interests.

Or, we want to be useful to the world, but the present chance to do good is not good enough, big enough or

71

ripe enough. We will wait and save our best thoughts and energies for a more worthwhile opportunity. Then, suddenly, we are at the end of our row, and our basket is empty.

One of life's most deceptive illusions is that the present moment is unimportant, the present opportunity to perform a kindness and render a service is a negligible one, the present decision is an indifferent one. We should plant deep in our minds the conviction that *this* day is the one day of which we are certain. Yesterday is but a memory, and tomorrow may never come. Today's energy is all we can count on; it is here. Yesterday's is depleted, and there is no guarantee of tomorrow.

The religious attitude toward life is that every day comes to us from God; that our preparation to serve the world, our talents and skills, are God's gifts; and every opportunity to use these talents and skills for good is also God-given. The person of faith does not claim to know what are the biggest and best opportunities. Such secrets are God's alone to keep. The faithful person does not wait for spectacular chances to make his influence felt. Instead, he performs everyday tasks as best he can. He is alert to ordinary human needs and commonplace opportunities to serve his generation.

He does not let *what he cannot do* get in the way of *what he can do*. As the man of faith moves along the rows of moments and days, he plucks every good chance to make his life an effective influence and does not wait for a *perfect* chance. He believes he is presently surrounded with opportunities to serve and spread joy. He can proclaim his faith and fulfill his highest purposes by doing his best with what lies nearest at hand.

The writer of the Acts of the Apostles characterized the Apostle Peter as a person who knew how to use whatever gifts he had, right where he was, rather than wishing he had other gifts to bestow at some other time in some more favorable place. In the third chapter of the Acts Peter is shown going with John to the temple to pray. While they were on their way they were stopped by a lame beggar who pleaded for money. Peter looked upon him with compassion and said, "Silver and gold have I none; but such as I have give I thee: In the name of Jesus Christ of Nazareth rise up and walk." And Peter lifted him to his feet, "and immediately his feet and ancle bones received strength."

Some disciples, if approached by someone requesting money, would give money or nothing. If they had no money it might never occur to them to give a healing touch of tenderness, an encouraging word, a few minutes of concerned listening to a recital of the man's woes — how he got that way, what sort of care he was receiving, his prospects for recovery, his chances for employment. The man asked for money; give him money or nothing! So we habitually respond to cries for help. But when Peter could not give what was requested, he gave what he could, the power of his faith. And it turned out to be a better blessing than all the money in Jerusalem.

The waste of life is found in giving nothing if we cannot give money, in doing nothing when we cannot do what we would like. Life is foolishly, wickedly squandered when the strong hand is not extended in help, when needed love is withheld, when the kind thought is unexpressed and the helpful word is unspoken. And such waste usually occurs when we wait for a better opportunity. Peter could have said, "I have no money right now. Perhaps I can return with some later." Instead, he gave what he could, then and there — the power of his compassion and faith.

Four centuries before Christ, the Greek poet Euripides advised, "Slight not what's near through aiming at what's far." Trying to refashion the entire world after your liking is an impossible and discouraging task. The effort will bring you down to the end of your days in defeat and bitterness. But even if you cannot remake the world to suit you, you can change the atmosphere of your immediate environment, bringing more joy to your family, your business and professional associates, your neighbors and friends. Now, right where you are, you can be more responsive to human need, more cheerful and charitable, more appreciative and grateful, more encouraging.

Like Peter, you can find someone right around the corner who needs your strong hand and faith if he is to stand on his feet and walk.

14

A Reverent Awareness Is the Root of Religion

When our pioneering forefathers first came to America they credited the Indians with phenomenal eyesight. An Indian could see a squirrel's eye where a white man saw only leaves, and a red man could spy a deer's antler in a hemlock thicket where a white man saw only the branch of a tree.

But as white men took to the woods and hunted like the Red Men they discovered their eyesight was as good as that of Indians. Indian eyes had never been physically better than the colonists' eyes; Indians simply knew what they were looking for and how to look. They were intent upon finding squirrels and not leaves, deer and not branches, and they would not let leaves and branches distract their attention from the game they were hunting. It was the Indian's interest rather than his visual aptitude that made him so keen-sighted. When white colonists developed the same interest, they found they had the same capacity for seeing.

-KOH

A man who spends his life on the high seas will be able
to see a warning buoy much sooner than one who spends
his days on land. His lifelong interest in buoys enables
him to focus attention upon them and to rule out all else.
The sailor's eyes and brain choose the buoys from all else
that distracts the landlubber's eyes, such as waves, low-
hanging clouds, sea birds, and sailing vessels.

In matters of religion, as everywhere else in life, the
secret of success is attentiveness based upon interest.
Such attentiveness saves us from the poverty of unaware-

ness. We go about the world unconscious of the goodness and glory that are all around us and unaware of the God who is near us. Perhaps it is because God is always near that we miss noticing Him until we are desperate for Him, much as we give little thought to our need of oxygen until we are gasping for air and threatened with suffocation. God may be excessively obvious as air is to man or as water is to fish.

Some anonymous poet has written:

> *"Oh, where is the sea?" the fishes cried,*
>   *As they swam the crystal waters through;*
> *"We have heard from old of the ocean's tide,*
> *And we long to look on the water's blue.*
>   *The wise ones speak of an infinite sea;*
>   *Oh! Who can tell if such there be?"*

Living in water, a fish might miss the meaning of water, while seeking its food and escaping its enemies. Living in God, we miss God while making a living, seeking our comforts and our pleasures.

The genius of early Hebrew religion was the way it impressed people with the presence of the Supernatural encompassing the natural, the nearness of the Eternal Spirit who sustains the world and all that is in it. Man might forget God, rebel and sin against God, but man could not escape the presence of God.

One lofty expression of this faith is found in the One Hundred and Thirty-ninth Psalm:

> *Whither shall I go from thy spirit? or whither shall*
>   *I flee from thy presence?*
> *If I ascend up into heaven, thou art there: if I make my*
>   *bed in hell, behold, thou art there.*
> *If I take the wings of the morning, and dwell in the*
>   *uttermost parts of the sea;*

77

> *Even there shall thy hand lead me, and thy right
> hand shall hold me.*

God knows us, but not from afar off as an American boy knows something about a pen-pal correspondent in India or Japan. God is with us. As Tennyson sang, "Closer is He than breathing, and nearer than hands and feet."

The religious person is one whose life is controlled by such an awareness of God. The man of faith believes that he lives out his days in the presence of God his Maker, and he acts as if God is always near and concerned with what that man is like, with what that man is doing, and with where that man is headed. This makes for disciplined living, for the more vivid our awareness of the presence of the good God, the better people we want to be. Some American Indians never wore a headdress, saying that they did not want their thoughts hidden from the Great Spirit. We believe that, headdress or no, all our thoughts stand naked before God. Therefore they should be clean, as should our deeds. An awareness of God is morally controlling.

A six-year-old girl engaged her father in a discussion about God. Instead of ending the conversation with a typical conclusion such as, "Daddy, I believe in God," or "Everyone should believe in God," she asked, "Daddy, could we invite God to spend the week end with us sometime?" Such a question plunges deep into the meaning of faith. It is more than a mere intellectual assent to the idea of God's existence. It gets to the heart of religion, which is an awareness of God as a Presence and a desire for fellowship with Him.

We must give our attention to God until the Eternal is so real to us and so desirable that we shall think of Him as the Presence abiding with us not only on weekends but throughout all our days.

15

Why Attend Church?

Going to church on a cold day in colonial times took courage and determined devotion. The distances across the chilled countryside were often great, and horse-drawn sleds sometimes took hours to reach the place of worship.

Upon arriving at the church the people were likely to be even more uncomfortable than while on their journey. In some New England churches it was regarded as sacrilege to have a stove in the church. Still other churches made no provision for heat because the deacons dreaded an accidental fire. Sometimes square pews were curtained off to keep out chilly drafts. Quilts, bearskins and even carpets were brought into the pews to fortify worshipers against the cold. Small, individual foot-stoves were used by the worshipers. Hot coals were fed into the little stoves for "Sabbath Day houses," which were small buildings near the churches with great fireplaces in the center. A caretaker kept the fire blazing so that churchgoers could replenish their foot-stoves. When the sanctuary was un-

- KOHN

bearably cold the worshippers slipped out of the church for a few minutes, stood near the roaring fire in the Sabbath Day house, and then returned to the worship service. Many an early preacher delivered his sermon with his overcoat and ear muffs on and a muffler over his head, and gestured with mittened hands.

Since the first church was established, there have always been some difficulties involved in going to church. Early Christians were under the suspicion of Roman authorities as trouble-makers and were also harassed by religious authorities. When their enemies wanted to discover and identify Christians they kept watch on their places of worship. Many Christians were tortured and killed. Others were imprisoned. But Christians continued attending services of worship, rejoicing through their sufferings.

Even when Christians have persecuted each other and have killed one another and destroyed one another's churches in the name of religion, the dangers of going to church have not halted church attendance.

In our own day we are less likely to be kept from church by cold sanctuaries or danger of persecution than we are by other interests. The chief competitors of the worship service today are late sleeping, later breakfasts, television, Sunday reading, the ski slopes, the golfing green and a host of other distractions.

Nevertheless, this week end there will be worshipers in virtually every temple and church throughout the world. Some churches will be packed with people, and some will have only a few; but wherever a service is held there will be some present who found it difficult to get there. Some are poor in health. A few have company they have to leave behind. Other interests and duties call persuasively to others. But in spite of all the excuses that could be given, many people still go to church. Why?

Millions attend public worship services because they wish to be led into the presence of the Most High and to be shown the meaning of life and the way to live better. The church is a place with a message. It bears the mighty reminders of whence we came, what we are, where we are headed, and what we can become, by God's grace. The church stirs conscience, offers insight and hope. In a time when the world is absorbed with Left and Right, the devout wish to be reminded that there is still an Above and a Below. The church bids us look up and say, "Our Father." It urges us to look out upon the world responsibly and with compassion. It points to Christ as Saviour and Standard of conduct.

Moreover, people go to church because this holy institution provides a regular time and place that is especially suited for worship. While we know God is with us in our homes, in our work and play, and while it is true that we can worship in places other than churches, the fact is that regular, sustained reflection upon life's greatest meanings is neglected unless we provide a certain time and a specific place for it. Even the streamside, the lakeside, the meadow and the forest, for all their revelation of God's wondrous handiwork, are not ideal for sustained worship. The distractions are too many. A bird's sudden flight, a fish's leap, a bounding hare or deer will interrupt one's thoughts and lead them away from worship. The church has walls and stained glass windows for shutting out distractions. And the hymns and Scriptures, prayers and sermons are designed to help keep one's mind centered on God.

Again, some people attend church because they believe it is not enough to sit in life's bleachers and "boo" at the mistakes or cheer over the successes of others who have chosen to do God's work. They know that religion is not a "spectator sport," but a "participant sport." The church gives us a chance to contribute our character, our strength and service to the cause that works for good will, peace, justice, righteousness and the common good.

A deaf-mute was once asked, "Why do you persist in going to church each Sunday when you cannot hear what is said or sung?"

The man wrote out his reply: "I go to church each week to let people know which side I am on."

The world is choosing sides between good and evil. Some people wisely attend church to show on which side they stand.

Finally, people have attended public worship because the church provides the place and occasion for fellowship with those who are going the same way. Worship, rightly used, unifies and strengthens. Each worshiper's faith is reinforced and supported by the faith of others.

The church, so far as it is loyal to the spirit of Christ, minimizes our differences and accents our oneness. In a divided world the church teaches men to say the unifying word "our" — "Our Father," "our daily bread," "our trespasses." It speaks of our common needs and the one answer who is God.

The historians tell us that when the Romans invaded Britain, the chiefs of the native tribes gathered in council. Each chief had a plan of his own for repelling the enemy; each was stubbornly insistent upon using his own plan for battle. When the council was hopelessly deadlocked, an old, wise, revered chieftain arose, picked up a bundle of sticks and handed a stick to each tribal chief. "Now, break them!" he ordered. Every man easily snapped his stick. Then the aged chieftain took an equal number of sticks, tied them in a tight bundle and said to the chiefs, "Break them now, if you can." Even the strongest man could not break the bundle of sticks. Then the wise chieftain said, "That is the difference between working separately and working together." And it is the difference, too, between "solitary religion" and the fellowship of faith within the church.

The great danger of the church today is not that it will be criticized, persecuted, or hounded to death; it has always thrived on opposition. The peril comes from the church's preoccupied and indifferent "friends," who believe worship is valuable but inconvenient.

Taking a journey through the week without "bothering" to stop for public worship is like trying to tour the United States without stopping at a gasoline station. We stall. The church is power for traveling.

See you in church!

16

We Are All Obedient

We commonly speak of obedience as a virtue to be found only among the good and the godly. But it is not. Obedience cannot be taken or left alone as we please. It is a law of life, more of a stark necessity than a chosen virtue. Everyone is obedient.

While we may glowingly say of a youngster who has pleased us, "He is such an obedient child," the fact is that every child is obedient. There is no such thing as a disobedient child, if you mean by "disobedient" a child who won't obey anyone or anything. The difference between a well-behaved and an unruly child is in *what* the children obey. Every child obeys something, if not his parents, then his instincts and his impulses. If he will not comply with the rules of deportment in school, he will submit to his own resentments against the authority of teachers, or to his wish to be considered smart or bold by his fellow students, or to his desire to be envied, or to his craving for attention, or to his yearning for revenge upon classmates who have offended him.

The sexually delinquent girl is obedient. She obeys her insatiable inner demands to be desirable, to "count" with someone, and she resigns herself to the impulses of the moment, thus mortgaging her entire future. But the chaste girl obeys an inner voice that bids her await the time when these urges and impulses can find a wholesome, unashamed expression within a marriage relationship. But both girls are obedient — to something.

A delinquent boy is on probation because he wants a gang of boys to know that he is daring enough to steal, and he obeys his own craving to be considered brave and clever in the eyes of the gang. Another juvenile protects, rather than pilfers, his neighbor's property in compliance with a high personal standard of conduct. Both are obedient boys.

The woman who whispers abroad her base opinions of others and enlarges upon their real and imagined faults is obedient to her desire to reduce others to her own level so that she can feel equal to them. But the woman who is tolerant and forgiving of another's faults is obedient, too — to high principles to which she has committed herself. So slander dies at her door.

The man who refuses to enter a burning building to rescue a screaming child obeys his instinct for self-preservation, and the other man who risks his life to save the child obeys the inner urge of his compassion. Both men are obedient. Everyone is — to something.

The Gospel of Matthew tells of Christ, on the night before His crucifixion, praying concerning His forthcoming ordeal, "My Father, if it be possible, let this cup pass from me; nevertheless, not as I will, but as thou wilt." Religionists have often pointed to this event as witness to Christ's obedience and have used it as a lesson to Christ's followers that they must emulate their Master in developing the virtue of obedience. That emphasis is a

mistaken one. Christ had no choice between being obedient and being disobedient. He was bound to obey. If He chose not to comply with the heavenly Father's will, still He would obey something, perhaps His natural wish to be well liked; thus He could muffle His message and make it pleasant to the ears of His listeners, and He could recant the disagreeable things that had irritated His enemies. Or Christ could obey an impulse to accept the acclaim and adoration that had been given Him in Jerusalem's streets on Palm Sunday, and then settle down comfortably as a local hero. But Jesus chose to be obedient to the highest He knew, the Father's will, so He prayed, ". . . Nevertheless, not as I will, but as thou wilt."

Christ's prayer is the summation of all true praying. It says what most needs to be said by every one of us — "Nevertheless not as I will, but as Thou wilt."

Only when man finds something which he obeys totally does life come into coherence and unity and find meaning. Groping for such a completeness, some people have turned to the totalitarianisms of their time, Fascism and Naziism a few years ago, and Marxism-Leninism in the past several decades; there they have found an allegiance to which they have given themselves totally. Evil often gets a following because it attracts those who feel "at loose ends" and crave a total obedience that will pull their lives together. But the good life, too, is lived in wholehearted obedience. The supreme reign of God over a person's entire life integrates desire, thought and action. It brings all the "tag ends" of life together. The rascals and the righteous, the sinners and the saints differ mainly in *what* they obey.

Read the letters early Americans wrote to their relatives and compatriots, and see how often they signed them "Your obedient servant." George Washington and Thomas Jefferson frequently signed their correspondence in this fashion, as did Abraham Lincoln sometime later. Henry David Thoreau, one of the most indomitable, independent spirits America has known, sometimes concluded his letters with the expression, "Yours to command."

Wouldn't the thoughts we send Godward, our prayers, bear more meaning if we concluded them with some such significant acknowledgment, "Your *obedient* servant?"

17

Obedience Is Power

In his address at the Federal Convention at Philadelphia in 1787, just before fixing his signature to the Constitution, George Washington declared, "Let us raise a standard to which the wise and honest can repair." Then he added, "The event is in the hands of God." While Washington believed that man should crave freedom, declare his rights to freedom, and fight and die for freedom, he knew that the final outcome of all man's strivings was in better hands than man's own. Washington saw that man's welfare and destiny rested in man's seeking and doing the will of God and not in getting God to do man's will.

It is good for all of us to be occasionally confronted by events that are plainly out of man's control. Perhaps one reason why some of us feel reverence mixed with our uneasiness when a winter storm descends upon us is that storms are events beyond man's command and mastery. Just now, outside the window where I sit writing, light

wanes and a cold day hardens into colder night. Whirl-pools of snowflakes, whipped by a northwesterly gale, swirl earthward in wild confusion. Driven by growling winds, snow piles in low mounds around my study window, heaping high on the sloping skirts of balsam, hemlock and spruce, where crouch the big-eyed hares and nestle the gem-eyed mice. The frostbitten foundations of our house are blanketed by billowing drifts.

Now a radio announcer begins his report of the changes Nature makes in man's plans. Meetings scheduled for this evening are being postponed or canceled. "The Cub Scouts will not meet with Mrs. B. tonight, because of the storm." "The Ladies' Auxiliary will postpone tonight's meeting until next Tuesday." "The Men's Club . . . ." "The West Side Association . . . ." And so it goes. This wintry onslaught covers much of the nation. Wind-chastened, cold-stiffened, snow-dazzled Northerners, Midwesterners and Southerners abandon all plans for the evening, excepting plans for keeping safe and warm.

Such a widespread, severe storm as this is a corrective for our egocentric tendencies. A blizzard may restore perspective. Man's boasted bigness and self-reliance are reduced to his real smallness and dependence. A man's ego shrinks in a storm, and he sees how dependent he is on the seasons, on the weather; how desperately necessary it is that he maintain his internal body temperature of 98.6 degrees.

It is good to be reminded that this is not a man-centered universe, that something bigger and more awesome is going on, other than tidy arrangements for man's convenience. My wish for a bright and sunny winter's day will not change the direction of the wind or diminish the force of the storm. And, thank God, my prayer that this blizzard will stop instantly, because I want to take a trip tonight, will likely be unavailing. If my whims could control the weather, God would cease being God. If He were honor-bound to answer all man's prayers, whims and wishes concerning blizzards, floods, testings and temptations, and all else we wish to avoid, man would control God and thus manage the universe. God would be slave to man's wishes.

Thank God that God remains God! And since He is God, the answers to our prayers must be *His* answers, not *our* answers thrust upon His lips. They must be His answers, in His time, backed by His wisdom and His concern for our needs. Neither our flimsiest fancies, nor our easy comfort, nor our pleasant conveniences are His great concerns. Our characters and eternal destiny are. An unwanted hardship may build more soul, and testing may strengthen more moral fiber, than all the pleasantness an easy life can afford us. Storms have a rightful place in this kind of world.

Again, a hammering gale frees us from our egocentric trap, because it shows us how inadequate are all man's boasted technological triumphs and infinitely varied inventions. Our audacious intention of mastering Nature seems strangely dimmed by a snowstorm sweeping out of the northwest. Tonight we are doing what man always has had to do, at last, if he was to survive; we are adjusting to Nature, which is our secularized way of saying "adjusting to God." We are learning which way the wind blows, how much snow can be expected, and how long the storm will last. And we shall prepare for the siege accordingly. In short, we shall learn and obey. We are not the center of everything. A force bigger than we are, a power that was here before we came and that will be here when we are gone, is expressing itself. We bend to it. We obey.

If we are to progress, or merely exist, in this world, this is how it will always be done — through obedience. We shall learn Nature's way and obey. We shall discover the Higher Will and follow it, having plumbed the meaning of Washington's trust, "The event is in the hands of God."

All of man's tall talk of "conquering Nature" is empty. Nature has never been conquered in its skirmishes with man. We but discover more about Nature and obey the "more" we have learned. All scientific advances are made in this manner. When heart disease and cancer eventually, if ever, become extinct, the triumph will not be affected by man gaining victory over Nature. Scientists will succeed because they have bowed humbly over sick bodies, over microscope slides and charts and records, and they have watched how disease works. They will learn the conditions under which these diseases prosper and the conditions which discourage or prevent them. Then, obeying Nature's clues, they will press forward in the war on disease. Nature will not be conquered, but some higher secret will be disclosed and some yet unknown law will be obeyed. In science, obedience is power.

A snowstorm reminds us of our real place in the world. We are not in charge! "The event is in the hands of God." We are not the Creator, but His creatures, not masters, but learners and servants. The chief aim of the soul is to learn the Higher Will and to do it.

Obedience is power.

18

The Inside Chores

Foul weather has frequently been the nursemaid of arts and skills. "Bad" weather forces people to withdraw for a while from the outer world and casts them upon their inner resources.

In the American yesteryears when bleak, snow-blown, icy January and February arrived, and winter lay stiff upon the windowpanes, and the rutted roads and paths were slippery with sparkling, quartzlike ice, and heavy snow stilled the wagons and made traveling difficult for horse and sled, then the farmers tended to their "inside chores." When they felt trapped by winter's wizardry of winds and cold our farming forefathers made adventures of their inconveniences.

In January and February the farmer went to his shop or forge-barn where he made some tools and repaired others, so that when spring came he was ready for the garden and the fields. The forge fire blazed hot and high as he fashioned plowshares, axe-heads, hoe blades and shovels. In colonial days landowners even made their own nails. During those early times in America nearly every farmer was his own blacksmith, and most of such work was done on stormy days when "outside work" was impossible.

Winter was also a time for making furniture, matching the seasoned woods in such a way that each kind of wood would work against the other, hard wood matched against springy wood, so that each tightened the other and the furniture could not fall apart. The homecraft of furniture-making was largely developed during uncomfortable winter weather.

Farm women used wintry days for candle-making, spinning, scouring pots and pans. Stormy days were just right

LATCHSTRING on a CABIN DOOR

for quilt-making, too. Our pioneering forebears well illustrated faith's victory over difficulties. They believed that when life was less than ideal and they could not do everything they liked, there were still worthwhile things that *could* be done, even on the worst days. They converted unpromising days into hours of creativity. They explored and exploited their harsh days by getting "caught up" and even ahead in the "inside chore" department of living.

Spiritually speaking, bad weather is a good time to do the inside chores. Basically, stormy days do one of two things to us and sometimes both: they reveal what is already in us, and, by God's grace, they transform us into something better than we are. In early America, on wintry days, doubtlessly some farmers went busily to work performing inside tasks while others insisted on doing outside work or nothing. On bad days the latter loafed. Thus storms revealed the character of the farmers, separating the benefactors from the bums. Then, again, every time a creative farmer was forced into his forge-barn or wood-working shop by inclement weather he gained more practice making tools and furniture. So stormy days sharpened a man's skills and improved the products of his mind and hands. Turbulent times reveal what we already are and change us for the better, if we will have it so.

Joseph is sold by his brothers into Egypt. Once a great man's son and now a slave — what an opportunity for sulking self-pity! But Joseph, who seems to have been something of a spoiled braggart, goes to work on his inside chores, examining his attitudes, tidying up his soul until his stay in Egypt makes him prime minister and the savior of his starving family who came to that land for help.

Alexander Pope once called his deformed body "a

bundle of distempers" and described his life as a long disease. Yet he so applied himself to creative thought and writing that his works have been enjoyed throughout the world and used as examples of a polished style in literature.

Immanuel Kant stands in the front ranks of the philosophers of all time, but it is believed that throughout his adult years he was never entirely free from pain. Much of his reflection was the result of deliberately withdrawing his attention from his ailments and concentrating on philosophical thought.

Henry Wadsworth Longfellow's beautiful translation of Dante has more meaning for us if we know that Longfellow's wife accidentally set her dress on fire, that the poet failed in his frenzied attempt to quench the flames, and that after she died of burns Longfellow attempted to comfort his broken spirit and occupy his stunned mind by translating Dante's work from the Italian.

Such souls as these have used wintry weather as a time for doing inside chores. They have made the most of unwanted situations.

Wild weather provides the occasion for straightening up the inner man, for reordering and polishing one's thinking and style of life, for discovering spiritual and moral weaknesses and taking steps to repair them. A stormy time offers opportunity to improve our aim in life, to re-evaluate and raise our purposes. Grief has shown many a man that he has taken for granted the presence and the love of those near him, and he has highly resolved never to do so again. Failure, disappointment, discouragement, sorrow and loneliness have proven to many how foolhardy it is for man to lean upon man's strength alone when we can rely upon the dependable power and goodness of the Eternal God, our Father. Thus calamity becomes the soul's opportunity.

Do you suppose that God allows some wintry blasts of trouble to enter our days because only then will we give attention to the inside chores?

19

A Willingness to Be Unpopular

Our American success standards include almost immediate and continuous public approval, and our modern heroes are those who rank highest in the popularity polls. Since this is so it would pay us to recall that the men whose lives have most influenced American history and who now are held in sacred memory and highest regard were not wholeheartedly approved or loved by their contemporaries. While they had a natural liking for public approval, they craved something else far more: personal integrity and an unsullied conscience. They concentrated on preparing for their great tasks and presenting their case in the most effective manner possible. Seeking to serve the common good of man, they appealed to the aspirations and hopes of their people. When they made mistakes, they amended them if possible (and often their enemies performed for them an unintended service in pointing out errors). But when their decisions proved unpopular and were harshly criticized,

100

our most esteemed leaders of the past did not sulk.
Nor did they strike back or live in a constant dither,
fearing for their reputations. Rather, they pressed on
toward their goals.

As the years pass, the world's esteem for Abraham
Lincoln has grown steadily until Lincoln has become
the most universally loved American of all time. But
we easily forget that during his administration as President of the United States he was the object of constant attack. President Lincoln could read, almost any
day he cared to take the trouble, scoffing criticisms
of his appearance and his grammar, malicious attacks
upon his character, or shockingly intemperate and hateful denunciations of his conduct in office. Less than a
year before Lincoln was assassinated, shortly after his
renomination as candidate for re-election and Andrew
Johnson's nomination as vice-presidential candidate, the
New York World published this evaluation of Lincoln
and his political partner:

"The age of statesmen is gone, the age of rail-splitters
and tailors, of buffoons, boors and fanatics, has succeeded.
. . . In a crisis of the most appalling magnitude, the country is asked to consider the claims of two ignorant, boor-
ish, third-rate backwoods lawyers, for the highest stations
in the government. . . . God save the Republic!"

Some of Lincoln's ambitious, jealous and greedy Cab-
inet members, seeking the Presidency themselves, sought
to undermine his influence, and gossiped about him
shamelessly.

Those of his countrymen who favored the immediate
abolition of slavery were impatient and critical because
Lincoln would not hurry the emancipation of the Ne-
groes as rapidly as they wished. (An abolitionist leader
once labeled him "The slave-hound of Illinois.") Those
opposing emancipation hated Lincoln because it ap-

101

You can have no conflict, without being yourselves the aggressors. You have no oath registered in Heaven to destroy the government, while I shall have the most solemn one to "preserve, protect and defend" it.

I am loth to close. We are not enemies, but friends— We must not be enemies. Though passion may have strained, it must not break our bonds of affection. The mystic chords of memory, stretching from every battlefield, and patriot grave, to every living heart and hearthstone, all over this broad land, will yet swell the chorus of the Union, when again touched, as surely they will be, by the better angels of our nature.

CLOSING PARAGRAPH OF LINCOLN'S FIRST INAUGURAL ADDRESS.
From original from which the address was delivered.

LINCOLN

peared he would free the slaves when he felt the time was ripe.

When circulars detrimental to the President were distributed throughout the country, many copies fell into the hands of Lincoln's friends and were brought to the White House. Nicolay, the President's secretary, revealed that Lincoln was wholly without curiosity concerning these attacks made upon him. He knew where the hate-filled circulars were piled, but refused to look at them.

In November, 1863, Abraham Lincoln spoke at the service dedicating the battlefield at Gettysburg, Pennsylvania, as a national cemetery. The compact, simple, sun-clear, two-minute speech has become one of the treasures of the English language, and although it was written without literary intent, the Gettysburg Address has become recognized the world over as deserving to be included with the great literature of all time. Yet Lincoln's words were mercilessly criticized in the newspapers of his day. The *Chicago Times* said of Lincoln's Gettysburg Address:

"The cheek of every American must tingle with shame as he reads the silly, flat, and dish-watery utterances of the man who has to be pointed out to intelligent foreigners as the President of the United States."

An American correspondent of the London *Times* declared that "the ceremony was rendered ludicrous by some of the sallies of that poor President Lincoln. . . . Anything more dull and commonplace it would not be easy to produce."

Abraham Lincoln once explained his attitude toward the criticism heaped upon him as follows:

"If I were to read, much less answer, all the attacks made on me, this shop might as well be closed for any other business. I do the very best I know how . . . the very best I can; and I mean to keep doing so until the end. If the end brings me out all right, what is said against me won't amount to anything. If the end brings me out wrong, ten angels swearing I was right would make no difference." At another time he declared, "I desire to so conduct the affairs of this administration that, when I come to lay down the reins of power, if I have lost every other friend on earth, I shall at least have one friend left — the one down inside of me."

Lincoln cared what people thought of him because he loved people, and he longed for a friendly response, but he cared without being anxious. As Ralph Waldo Emerson one time said, "The solar system has no anxiety about its reputation." Neither had Lincoln.

Abraham Lincoln shared to a great degree the criticism that his hero, George Washington, had borne to a lesser extent. While many of Washington's contemporaries recognized his greatness, there were others who treated him with ill-concealed contempt. They peddled untrue stories about his personal habits. One day after Washington retired from the Presidency, one of the leading newspapers in the new country said that if "ever there was a period for rejoicing, this is the moment. Every heart ought to beat high with exultation that the name of Washington from this day ceases to give currency to political iniquity and to legalized corruption." Joy was expressed that "the man Washington is this day reduced to a level with his fellow citizens and is no longer possessed with power to multiply evils upon the United States."

If Washington and Lincoln had been given a clear and simple choice between being popular everywhere or being angrily and bitterly denounced by some, doubtlessly they would have chosen universal approval. But life offers no such choices to the useful person. Universal and uninterrupted approval is impossible for the serviceable person to achieve. To count for good and for God in the world a person must want to be useful more than he wants to be popular. He may prefer to be liked but be willing to be disliked, if necessary, while he works on toward his high purposes. If he is fruit-bearing, he must expect stones and sticks will be thrown at him. There are few better tests of a person's character than the way he accepts criticism.

Abraham Lincoln amazed his critics by thanking them when he felt their criticism was just and constructive, by asking them for specific recommendations of where he could improve himself or his work, and by ignoring their censure where it was born of ill will.

An ultrasensitive thin-skinned America that appears to be engaged in a popularity contest with Soviet Russia and is easily hurt by criticism in the foreign press could well learn a lesson from Lincoln on the value of choosing the right over approval. So could our politicians (it might make statesmen of them!), and so could every citizen among us.

If we will do nothing until we can do it so perfectly that no one can find fault with it, we will do nothing at all. And to do nothing is the greatest of all human faults.

20

The Power of Waiting

Late spring is a time of waiting. The spading of gardens was done many weeks ago. Seeds have been planted. Rich, black soil now covers the slumbering life in all those hard-shelled little possibilities that men buy in packages. Now, excepting for a bit of weed-pulling, we must wait. Let the dark, rainy nights, bright mornings, glad, golden afternoons and dewy evenings nourish the seeds in their beds. Let breezes caress tiny plants; let the warm sun bless them and all the laughing hours of springtime enliven and refresh them. Let golden bees and emerald hummingbirds casually visit them as they go about their chores. And let the seeds and seedlings alone until they have a chance to grow.

Man is capable of gardening not only because he has the intelligence and the tools to plow or spade, to plant and hoe, to cultivate and to harvest, but because man has the power to wait for his expectations to be realized and for his desires to be satisfied. He can plant seeds in April

SUSANNA WESLEY

or May and harvest the plants in mid-summer or early fall and refuse to pull them up in the meanwhile to see if they are growing well enough to suit him. He can await the results of his best endeavor.

The lower creatures seek a more immediate satisfaction. One-celled amoebae bump into their food and consume it at once. They do not anticipate food or know any period of suspense between sensing the presence of food and devouring it. The cat will not and cannot wait a full day for a certain mouse to show its face and become a meal. A dog or a bull or a ram will not court a female of its species for months or years before mating. The lower animals are incapable of waiting for final satisfaction of their desires and impulses.

Man's power of waiting makes for much of his misery and his glory. If he could only take at once what he wants or ignore his wishes altogether he might be as comfortable as an amoeba. But then, again, he would also be as insignificant. He knows that all his enjoyments are but fragmentary; he hungers for a fulfillment that cannot be realized at once, and he strives for achievements that are long in coming.

The artist delights in his painting, but his pleasure is only fractional, for he must await the effect of slow, painstaking toil upon his work of art before he can know fulfillment. Impatient haste spoils everything of beauty. When Leonardo da Vinci was painting his "Last Supper" he was criticized for frequently standing for hours before the picture without making a single stroke with his brush. Leonardo would reply: "When I pause the longest, I make the most telling strokes." Such pauses are a creative kind of waiting: it is the sort of waiting that brings beauty into being.

We need such patient pauses in dealing with our children. We plant a lesson or an admonition or what we deem a good idea in a child's mind, and we expect an immediate harvest. The harvest better come today, or tomorrow at the very latest. Too often we provide no patient pauses for letting the idea germinate, sprout and grow. John Wesley's father once demanded of his wife: "How could you have the patience to tell that blockhead the same thing twenty times over?" Mrs. Wesley replied, "If I had told him but nineteen times, I should have lost all my labor." She knew that her admonitions and corrections must be given time to grow and ripen.

The power of waiting is greatly needed in every kind of healing, both physical and spiritual. How hard it is to endure prolonged bed rest when one is ill. If we then give in to fretfulness, restlessness, complaints or self-pity, our poor emotional health will frustrate healing. Impatience augments the illness. We need to understand that the Divine Healer works with doctors and nurses and with all those who are devoted to the healing arts, but He takes His time. The Great Physician cannot be pushed or rushed. The ill need to wait in quiet restfulness.

Emotional wounds must be treated with patience. They take time to heal. When we have forgiven those who have offended and hurt us and some attempt has been made toward reconciliation, when we have weeded out evil and have sown the good, then we must expect a creative pause before desired results can be seen. Feelings of shame, guilt, hurt and resentment do not die at the roots as soon as these weeds are pulled. And feelings of forgiveness, restoration and goodwill do not sprout and bloom the day they are planted. But God and time are inseparable partners and undiscourageable co-workers. They will work together. Give God time.

God's patient dealings with things of earth should teach us to be more patient with ourselves, and God's patience with us should teach us to be more patient with each other.

"They that wait upon the Lord shall renew their strength," said Isaiah. We could all use more of the power of creative waiting.

21

Remember the Scars

We remember what is most important to us. A woman who complained that she suffered from "a terrible memory" once told Dr. Bruno Furst, the noted authority on memory training, a harrowing tale of a memory lapse. She said she once was engaged to address a crowd of businessmen and women. She arrived late at the meeting because she had forgotten the name of the hotel. The names of the important people present at the meeting somehow eluded her memory, and when she rose to speak she couldn't recall what she had planned to say.

Dr. Furst asked what she had worn to that occasion, and she quickly responded, "My navy silk-shantung suit, my white straw hat and navy leather bag with shoes to match."

Can any woman who loves clothes forget what she has worn on her big occasions?

A little boy may forget to wash behind his ears, but he clearly remembers a promise of a picnic you made three weeks ago. He does not forget, either, when and where his gang will hold their next sand-lot baseball game.

If we can readily recall what is most important to us, why do we need special days of commemoration such as Christmas, Easter, Thanksgiving Day? Could we not remember Christ's birth and resurrection without a special day? Would we never give thanks without Thanksgiving Day? Why do we observe a special Memorial Day each springtime? Would we entirely forget our heroic dead if we did not decorate the graves of fallen soldiers, sailors, marines, and airmen on Memorial Day? Special days of commemoration are established so that all people might, on the same occasion, lift their hearts together in memory for some event. The difference between individual, occasional remembrance and a holiday celebration is like the difference between solos sung softly to ourselves while we work or play, compared with joining in a mighty choir. Such a choral concert is not intended to take the place of private humming and singing. But a choir concert provides a time and a place and the occasion for raising our voices in more glorious song than any of us could perform by ourselves.

So with Memorial Day: it is a time of concerted remembering, when millions pool their tenderest recollections, their gratitude for the sacrifices the dead have made for our safety, and their pledges of loyalty to the ideals for which those who sleep have died.

Now comes another Memorial Day. How, then, shall we venerate the dead of past wars with an honor that reaches beyond monuments, wreaths, wordy praise, and even tears? How shall we remember them?

Remember: They died in hope of bringing peace to the world. Above the graves of those slain in many wars we should refresh our resolution to do away with all war, with the hatreds that inspire it, with the bloodshed, pain, maiming and death, and countless other curses that attend it.

111

GENERAL GORDON

Remember: in every war we give our best men and women, not our worst. Only those who can pass the physical and mental tests are crippled and slain. Only those capable of dreaming great dreams and achieving great goals are sent to the sacrifice.

Remember the brevity of their lives before they were bruised and broken by war. Remember that the tragedy of war can be found not only in what happens to soldiers, sailors, and airmen, but in what *does not* happen to them. When they are cheated of their lives by war, some budding talents will never flower upon the earth. Some music will not be sung. Some inventions will not be made. Some books will not be written. Some cures for disease will be delayed in coming. Some women will go unloved. Some bright sons and daughters will not be born. When they were laid in their graves the unrealized possibilities of our young heroes were interred with them.

Remember: when heroes fight for what is right, we must not let the peace degenerate into a quarrel over what is left.

112

Remember to honor those who died for freedom by *being free*, by exercising conscience freely, by speaking freely in support of great causes, by voting freely, and always, on great issues.

Remember those who died that peace might come, by living peaceably with your family, neighbors and with other races and nationalities. Let honor be expressed in deeds.

Remember: the fairest flowers laid upon a grave are no substitute for a frequent kind word of appreciation to those who are still alive and with us and whose small sacrifices for our welfare should be recalled on Memorial Day and all other days. Let them know how much they mean to you before they, too, are gone.

A few years after the close of the Civil War, General John B. Gordon became a candidate for the United States Senate from the state of Georgia. In those days senators were elected by the state legislature. An old soldier who had been a comrade of General Gordon and who had taken a strong dislike to him was serving in the Georgia legislature when the vote on Gordon's candidacy was taken. He had determined to vote against the general.

The vote was taken by roll call, and General Gordon was on the platform where he could watch the proceedings. When the old soldier's name was called, he rose to his feet and was about to cast his vote against the general. But his eyes fell on Gordon's face, and he saw the ugly battle scar that witnessed to the general's courage and suffering. The old soldier hesitated. Then, his voice choked with emotion, he said, "I cannot vote against him. I had forgotten the scar."

Memorial Day reminds us of all who have toiled, fought, and suffered for us. Every day should be hallowed by memorial moments when we remember the scars.

22

Convictions and Conduct

We frequently hear someone say, "It doesn't matter what you believe, as long as you believe in *something*." This statement is meant to stamp the speaker with two noble attributes: he is a person of faith, and he is broad-minded. Perhaps he is both, and yet either characteristic is insufficient in itself. While such a declaration seems like a statement of faith, it merely denotes *faith in faith* itself, and not faith in anything higher, deeper and more lasting than a person's belief. It means only that one believes in belief. It is a broad statement, too, broad like a certain swamp I know, where the water spreads for miles but is only a few inches deep. The idea that belief has value apart from the object of one's belief is a swampy shallow idea. For even a moment's thought will lead one to conclude that it does matter tremendously what one believes.

Let us briefly examine this widely held idea that what we believe matters little as long as we believe in some-

WHITMAN

thing. Is there any difference between snake-handling as an act of worship and Holy Communion as a sacrament? Of course there is, and the difference springs from a dissimilarity in belief. The snake handler is convinced that he is indulging in a valid way of testing and proving the strength of his religious faith. His belief prompts his weird action. The communicant at the Lord's Supper believes that through sacred memories, glad thanksgiving, solemn and sincere consecration and the use of holy emblems he is partaking of genuine fellowship with God in Christ. His belief prompts his participation in the sacrament. The snake-handling ceremony and the rite of Holy Communion are different in quality. The snake handler and the communicant behave differently because they believe differently.

115

Again, is there any difference between the behavior of George Custer toward the American Indians and the conduct of Marcus Whitman towards members of the same race? In 1868 Major General George A. Custer headed an expedition against Indian Chief Black Kettle, who claimed to want peace with the whites. Custer and his men totally wiped out the Indian village and without any discrimination massacred men, women and little children. (Thus Custer and his men repeated an atrocity committed nine years before by white men under the command of William Dame and Isaac Haight. This band of whites attacked a settlement of Indians and murdered one hundred and twenty men, women and children.) Isn't there a clear difference between such atrocities and the gentle, kindly care given to Indians of the West Coast by the missionary doctor Marcus Whitman and his wife Narcissa? The Whitmans eased the pains and healed the diseases of red men, and taught them to read and write, until they met their deaths at the hands of hostile braves. Custer and Whitman treated the Indians differently, because they thought of them differently. Whitman

placed a high value on an Indian's worth. What Custer and Whitman believed did make a difference.

Everyone agrees that what we do with our lives matters a great deal. What we believe matters then, too, because what we do depends upon what we believe. We shall behave selfishly or unselfishly, hatefully or helpfully, purposively or aimlessly, hopelessly or hopefully, depending upon whether we believe in an I-centered world or a God-centered universe; whether we believe that others are against us or others need us; whether we believe that life here is senseless or meaningful; whether we believe that ultimately man's wickedness or an unfeeling and uncaring fate rules the world, or that a loving God does; whether we believe we are the creatures of a moment or we were meant for eternity. Action springs from basic belief. We shall act one way or another because we believe one way or another. Thus, belief matters.

During World War I Theodore Roosevelt rediscovered how belief and behavior belong to each other. Roosevelt was proud of his three sons who had served their country during the early days of America's participation in the

CUSTER

war. But like all other parents Roosevelt was apprehensive concerning the safety of his children. One evening during the war the former President and his wife were sitting in their living room when a telegram arrived from the Roosevelts' fourth son, Quentin, informing his parents that he had enlisted in the air corps. Roosevelt was deeply troubled by the news and sat in brooding silence. Finally Mrs. Roosevelt spoke to him saying, "Colonel, you cannot teach your boys to believe like eagles and then expect them to act like sparrows." Of course not. Belief and behavior belong together. Men behave courageously when they possess courageous convictions. Those who have fought bravely in war, or against war, have possessed beliefs that made them brave. It matters what a person believes.

An almost illiterate backwoods preacher is said to have stated the two essentials of the gospel as "believing it and behaving it."

We will "behave it" better when we believe it profoundly enough.

23

What Do You Think of Yourself?

These are tough days for developing and maintaining our self-respect. It may be that feelings of self-worth are harder to come by now than at any other time in history. Our expanding knowledge of the size of the universe, our technology, the dominance of the machine that is more efficient than its maker, the towering problems of international relations and world order and the threat of man's self-annihilation all tend to dwarf man in his own sight and diminish his self-regard.

In the past we have enjoyed some natural aids to self-respect. Once upon a time most children in America felt needed. The role a child filled on the farm was an important one and he knew it. Even a three-year-old could help his parents by carrying light kindling wood or corncobs into the house so that his mother could start a fire in the cook stove. In a few more years the child could go to the far pasture after the cows, feed the calves and assist with the milking. He helped plant, cultivate and

harvest crops. A child knew that if he did not do his share of the farm chores the farm and family would suffer. He knew he was important.

But in this generation only an extremely small percentage of American children have the good fortune to grow up where they feel desperately needed. If they have any household chores to perform, the jobs are seldom the sort that seem significant. The very existence of the family does not depend upon their hard work. Thus, during the most impressionable years of their lives children are too easily led to believe that they are not very important, and their feelings of self-respect are damaged.

Moreover, from their earliest days many children's ears are assaulted with complaints about how much it costs to keep them supplied with shoes, clothing, play space, baby sitters, summer-camping experiences, education. They hear how much bother children are to parents, teachers, policemen, city planners. Children come to feel they are not worthy human beings but problems and nuisances. Is it any wonder they have trouble developing self-respect?

Self-respect is a prime necessity for wholesome living. Without it we lack the confidence to live life openly, courageously, venturesomely. We are afraid the world will discover what we are really like. We live clumsily, tensely, hesitatingly; we are self-reproachful and defensive. And, because we cannot respect ourselves, we do not respect others enough. We tend to disparage them and "cut them down" to our size so that we can feel more comfortable in their presence. But if a person has self-respect, and if it is firmly based on a conviction of man's dignity as a child of God, the world cannot take his self-regard from him.

Dr. Oliver Wendell Holmes was short in stature but tall in spirit. One time he attended a gathering where he was by far the shortest man present. An acquaintance jokingly asked Dr. Holmes if he did not feel small and insignificant in a crowd of big men, and Holmes answered, "Indeed I do! I feel like a dime in a collection of pennies!" No one could make Dr. Holmes think of himself as of no account. He was aware that his worth depended upon more than his height.

Without such feelings of self-esteem, the high regard of others counts for little. No one can enjoy the respect he receives from others unless he has self-respect. A person must feel he is somewhat deserving of the respect others show him; otherwise he will suffer from secret guilt because he believes he has fooled his friends and

121

acquaintances and has cheated them. He will believe that others do not really respect him at all; they respect the person they *believe* him to be. So the person who is without self-respect cannot fully savor the respect of others, no matter how enthusiastically they seem to approve and applaud him.

What is the religious basis for high self-regard? It is the conviction that everyone is created by God, is important to God, is loved by God. It is the belief that if we count so much with God, we ought to count with ourselves.

The early Christians had a high opinion of themselves. "Do you not know that your body is the temple of the Holy Spirit within you . . . ?" Paul asked the Corinthians. "See what love the Father has given us, that we should be called children of God; and so we are," declares the First Epistle of John. You deserve to be respected, especially by yourself. God has given you a good name, His family name. You are a "child of God," so the early Christians were taught to believe.

Say it to yourself: "I am a child of God. I did not make myself this way. God made me His child."

Make the thought habitual. Repeat it daily, "I am a child of God."

Live up to it.

Live in the excitement, the joy and the power of it.

Have a high opinion of yourself.

24

God Only Knows

An expression that is commonly spoken lightly (and ungrammatically) has profound religious significance when more seriously used: when a problem transcends understanding, a person is likely to say, "God only knows the answer to that!" Few utterances have more meaning to the life of faith than this, although it is often employed as half-oath or half-jest — "God only knows!" Life is packed with mysteries, and the humble person finds the words "I do not know" coming easily to his lips. But "I do not know" is not a religious affirmation unless coupled with its counterpart, "But it is known," or better yet, "God knows."

"God only knows" what is within us. We don't. Even the wisest person's inner nature is partially veiled from his own sight. The German philosopher Arthur Schopenhauer was walking one day along a promenade at Frankfort on the Main, accompanied by his little poodle dog. An English tourist eyed him curiously, wondering who the

SCHOPENHAUER

absent-minded, eccentric old gentleman might be. At last, unable to hold off any longer, the traveler approached the old philosopher and demanded, "Tell me, who in heaven's name are you?" Schopenhauer's half-humourous, half-pathetic reply was, "Alas, I wish I knew!" The Englishman thought the elderly thinker must be insane. But Schopenhauer was merely being honest.

None of us knows just who and what he is — not completely. This is particularly true of our possibilities. "God only knows" what they are. We know something about our achievements after possibilities have come to fulfillment; but those hidden forces within us that lie undeveloped, "God only knows" what they might be. Often potentials for good come to the surface through trouble, in much the same way that some islands are created in the midst of the sea. Deep beneath the tossing waters unseen forces are at work, restless, shifting about. Then, with-

124

out warning, a great rumbling runs through the earth beneath the sea. The very core of the world shakes and trembles. The earth opens and lava in molten or cinder form erupts, piling up from the sea floor until such islands as those found in Hawaii, the West Indies and the Azores are formed.

In a similar manner the power of God moves through the hidden urges and deeply buried possibilities of His people, disturbing them. Then, like an island uplifted above the sea, an unimagined goodness or an unexpected touch of greatness breaks into view. We see but the final result, the splendid character, or the towering Christ-like deed. But the possibilities that eventuated in those results — ony God knew about them.

Again, "God only knows" the extent of our influence. Some of us are suffering from rankling feelings of futility. We have tried to live good lives and make some differences in the world, but we can see no real results. We wonder if our efforts and good deeds were not wasted. Would our community not be just about the same if we had never lived there? What's the use of trying, when it all seems so futile? "God only knows!"

One vital answer to our feelings of futility is that our influence is accomplishing the most good when it is not visible, when it is hidden from our sight. The self-conscious "do-gooder," who is constantly parading his superior wisdom and his superlative morals and calling attention to his matchless dedication and his peerless deeds, seldom achieves the good results he expects and for which he labors. He repels more people than he helps. But the world's rich deposits of good are laid down by those who are simply going about seizing immediate and small opportunities to be helpful, not realizing the greatness of their performance. In fact, many of the world's great people have felt they were failures.

Our best influences are poured upon our time much as water is given to a dry and wilting plant. While the water is visible, it is doing the plant little good. But after the water disappears from sight and oozes down around the tiny root hairs, the plant is refreshed and revived. So with the good you have done and will do: you cannot see it at work. "God only knows" where your efforts have gone and what they are doing. But some day, somewhere, somehow, someone will be better because you have lived.

God knows!

25

Making a Living and Making a Life

An explorer of the Upper Amazon forests attempted a tough, three-day forced march through thick jungles, urging his hired porters to make good time in spite of discouraging difficulties. On the first and second days the carriers cheerfully obeyed his orders, and made extraordinary speed. But on the third morning when orders were given for the day's march to begin, the natives refused to move. The command was given again, but they would not budge. At last their chief explained their reluctance: "They are waiting for their souls," he declared. "They cannot travel further until their souls have caught up with their bodies."

There is more truth than superstition in the natives' decision to wait, for our bodies *do* outdistance our souls. Our work gets ahead of our spirits. Inspiration stops, but perspiration continues. We go through the motions of our tasks, lifting our burdens, bearing our responsibilities, keeping our promises, and meeting our engagements after we have forgotten the significance of it all.

With all our success in devising labor-saving gadgets that minimize the necessity for extreme physical exertion, "work" is still a curse-word to many a modern man. Could it be that by merely providing better *external* conditions for labor even the simplest tasks remain slavish unless we recognize our souls' involvement in our work? Is it enough to reduce all forms of compulsion, lessen discomfort and fatigue, provide coffee breaks, and raise wages, if the worker still feels that the task he performs counts for little or nothing?

It is easy to love sanitation and to believe in sewage systems, but it's hard to love ditch-digging or to believe in its dignity. Yet sanitation and ditch-digging are part of the same scheme of things, and the chief difference between ditch-digging as drab drudgery and ditch-digging as significant work lies in the meaning one sees in the ditch. Even shoveling holes can be done with distinction when the soul is involved, when the man with the spade sees his effort as affecting the health of a community.

Men of faith have always seen the soul's deep involvement in work done by the body. They have known that it is not enough to serve an employer unless one also serves a purpose. To be the servant of the Highest, no

matter who pays the wage, is to make a life as well as to make a living.

Many centuries ago the Psalmist pleaded in the Nine-tieth Psalm, "Let thy work appear unto thy servants, and thy glory unto their children. And let the beauty of the Lord our God be upon us: and establish thou the work of our hands upon us; yea, the work of our hands estab-lish thou it." *There* was a man who had allowed his soul to catch up with his work! He knew that spiritless, mean-ingless work is ugly drudgery, but when man's labor is seen in connection with God's work, it has rich signifi-cance. If God is Creator, then whenever we produce good, we are co-creators with Him, as is the farmer devel-oping a fallow field into a crop-yielding plot. Such work provides a fellowship with God, the ceaselessly toiling En-ergy that labors for the good of His children. The tiller of soil is co-creative with God in feeding the world's hun-gry. The carpenter is partner with God in sheltering man's fragile frame from the elements. The road builder, plane builder, and ship builder, the automobile and loco-motive manufacturers hold partnership with Him who wants all man to behave as brothers, and these make pos-sible the communication without which brotherhood is impossible. Those mining coal and drilling for oil, those tending nets on the high seas and reaping grain in harvest fields, those delivering milk at stores and doorsteps, those baking bread or freezing vegetables, delivering babies and doctoring the sick, teaching the young and comforting the aged — all these and nameless others, too, are God's associates in creating and sustaining His world.

When our souls catch up with our bodies then we see, as did the Psalmist, that "thy work" and "the work of our hands" belong together. Then work and worship blend.

26

A Look at Bigger Things

Religious faith gives us a sense of proportion and value. The very first of the Ten Commandments is aimed at establishing what must be highest in our system of priorities: "You shall have no other gods before me." The Eternal God comes first. All other matters are of secondary importance, at best.

We get into serious trouble whenever we disarrange the Biblical code of values, making other interests superior to God's interests and allowing secondary matters to be our primary concerns. Then our sense of self-esteem is diminished because the goals with which we identify ourselves are not worthwhile. Again, if our loyalties are given to little things instead of to the Highest, we become most affected by minor matters. A mere whim seems like a craving need that demands satisfaction at all costs. Small irritations seem like major catastrophes. Little disappointments bring on big emotional upsets.

A court case tried in England some years ago illustrates how looking at bigger things restores our perspective. Lord Beaverbrook, the British newspaper publisher, had been sued for libel by a certain Lady Terrington. She claimed that Beaverbrook's *Daily Express* had criticized her clothes, and as a result her reputation had been irreparably hurt. The lady asked for an exorbitant settlement in return for the damages.

Beaverbrook was defended by the brilliant barrister Sir Edward Marshall Hall. Sir Edward shrewdly timed the concluding phase of the trial so that it fell on Armistice Day and arranged that the two minutes of national silence in honor of the war dead would fall during his summation of the defense. When the hour of eleven o'clock struck, Sir Edward was in the midst of an impassioned statement of his client's innocence, but he broke off the argument, and the court was awesomely silent while all present stood for two minutes with heads bowed in tender memory. Then Sir Edward resumed his argument, solemnly saying, "Members of the jury, we have just commemorated our greatest national sacrifice. We have all suffered grievous losses in the war." Then Sir Edward wheeled upon the plaintiff and his voice rose in indignant accusation: "Now we turn from the painful remembrance of our heroic sacrifices to the trifling grievances of this lady."

Lady Terrington withered. So did her case. The lady did not receive a farthing. Her vanity could not endure the test of being set in perspective against the vast heartache of Englishmen, their Allies, and their enemies.

A look at bigger things should be a daily habit, and would cure many of us of our fretfulness over trifles. We would be less irritable, less captious, if we would lift our attention to eternal things and to the Eternal One, and thus correct our perspective.

Do we ever scold a child and send him off to school
bewildered and hurt simply because we spent a restless
night or because the breakfast toast was burned? Isn't the
loss of one night's sleep or a charred piece of bread a
pitifully small thing when compared to a child's self-
respect, his feelings of worth, and his craving to be loved?

We raise havoc with our marriages when we lose our
perspective. Then incidental frustrations are treated as
disasters. Fault-finding follows. Accusations and counter-
accusations leave open, festering psychological wounds.
A marriage partner tends to withdraw from the person
who hurt him. The wedded need to lift their eyes daily
to the big thing in their relationship — concern for each
other's happiness and welfare. All else then seems small.

Sometimes a crisis corrects our perspective. Then the
little things that have masqueraded as giants shrink to
their true proportions, and the big things that we have
minimized are seen to be very great indeed. A father
has told that his three small children once violently quar-
reled over some trifle just before bedtime. They were sent
to their rooms still complaining about each other and
muttering their grievances. But finally they fell asleep.
Shortly after midnight a storm began brewing, and by
two o'clock in the morning a terrifying thunderstorm
broke, with weird flashes of lightning brightening the

sky and deafening rolls of thunder shaking the house. The father heard the sound of shuffling little feet upstairs and called out, asking what the children were doing. A little voice tremulously answered, "We're all here in the clothes closet, forgiving each other!" When their small world seemed to be doomed, "forgiving each other" was what was most important to those quarrelsome children. Danger corrected their perspective, compelling them to look at bigger things.

I am not as pessimistic as many are about the future of the world, and I do not predict the imminent destruction of the earth by nuclear explosion. Nevertheless, these are dangerous days, and the best informed people of our time are the most frightened. They know our capacity to precipitate a final calamity. If the ultimate catastrophe seemed about to occur, wouldn't we be like those children, huddled together in reconciliation and forgiveness? And if these things are big enough to die by, are they not good enough to live by? Individually and internationally, forgiveness and reconciliation are too important to be saved for use in case of impending doom. These values which loom so large when disaster threatens should be treated as significant in everyday life.

God first! He deserves our primary devotion in crisis or calm. A daily look at the Highest and Best puts all other values in their proper places.

27

Hatred Hurts the Hater

Luther Burbank, the American naturalist and experimenter with fruits, vegetables and flowers, was once conversing with a friend concerning observations Burbank had made of the outstanding characteristics of plants, animals and children. He said that the chief trait of monkeys is their mania for tearing things to pieces. They have a deep-seated impulse to destroy and will pull apart anything they are strong enough to demolish — food, magazines, books. They are blind to worth; they cannot distinguish the value of one thing from another. Then the naturalist went on to liken gossips and critics to these creatures, declaring that they possess this monkey characteristic: they enjoy tearing people and reputations apart. And, like monkeys performing at a zoo, the gossips and critics usually have an audience which is bemused at their antics.

Hatred is an emotion that makes a monkey of man. The object of hatred is destruction. Whether we con-

sider the tiny seeds of hostility that are found in feelings
of irritation and revulsion, or we think of the full-grown
malevolence expressed through murderous rage or in a
wholesale war, hatred spreads ruin. In its most spectacular forms it kills people, and in more subtle ways it ruins
reputations, erects barriers between individuals and nations, destroys co-operation and worthwhile social inter-
action. But, especially, hatred harms the person who
harbors it.

The New Testament First Epistle of John declares,
". . . He who hates his brother is in the darkness, and
does not know where he is going, because the darkness
has blinded his eyes." Hatred is blindness, self-imposed.

Hatred prevents us from seeing how it is hurting us. In
the old Amos and Andy radio show there appeared a giant
of a character who loved to give Andy a friendly, enthusi-
astic slap across the chest whenever the two chanced to
meet. Andy wearied of the man and his vigorous swats, and
he confided to Amos a plan to discourage the big fellow's
habit. "I'm al set for him. I stuck a stick of dynamite in
my vest pocket. The next time he thumps me on the chest,
he's going to get his hand blown clean off!" Poor Andy!
He was too dull to realize that the explosion that would
destroy another's hand would shatter his own heart.

It is always so. Hate hurts the hater as well as the hated, but it keeps a person so intent upon seeing and punishing the evil in another that one is oblivious to what is happening to oneself.

Every schoolteacher has encountered a student who stubbornly refuses to prepare his lessons because he dislikes the teacher or hates school. He believes that he is defeating the teacher and the school administration if he refuses to study. He may have some subversive effect upon the classroom and the school, but the effect upon the pupil is positively ruinous. He cuts himself off from all manner of appreciations and opportunities that only a sound education can afford him. Thus he punishes himself, defeats himself, and becomes his own victim.

The hostile person kills his marriage by belittling, disparaging, nagging his partner, but it is *his* marriage as well as his mate's that he is hurting. The employee or employer who is ready to take offense and to exaggerate little disputes, quick to sulk, and hasty to retaliate pollutes the atmosphere of his own daily work with his attitude. He then must live in that suffocating influence. But he will blame others, not seeing himself as being at fault. Hatred blinds us to how much we hurt ourselves.

Hatred restricts our outreach. This blinding sickness makes shut-ins of all who contract it. They become isolated from all the good that is in the lives of those they intensely dislike. If we moderately dislike a person we may be almost indifferent to him, but if we dislike him intensely enough we begin to take a perverse interest in him, in his faults, failures and downfall. But at the same time we do not like to learn of his virtues, successes and triumphs. We ignore them if we can. Thus a whole range of experience with others is closed to us, that of seeing, admiring and emulating the best in another person.

Rudyard Kipling had a brother-in-law who was a most likable man, and Kipling and this in-law were good friends. But they became lifelong enemies when the brother-in-law drove his wagon in such a way as to cause Kipling to fall off his bicycle. Both became shut off from the good in the life of the other.

Gilbert and Sullivan, of light-opera fame, once had a falling out over the price of a carpet and were never again on friendly terms, although they continued to collaborate on the composition of operas. They were shut-ins, isolated from the great good in each other by their malice.

Two of the greatest baseball heroes of all time, who played on the same team, had a misunderstanding over a remark made by one concerning the dress the other titan's daughter was wearing. For years they did not speak to each other excepting in the performance of duty. Only near the end of their careers, when one of them was taken critically ill, did they reconcile. In the meantime they suffered a hate-blindness that kept each from seeing the other for the great man he was.

How many adventures in friendship and appreciation we miss because we are restricted by a hostility-induced blindness.

Hatred impairs health. Clinical findings have proved long ago that inner tensions, as well as organic diseases, precipitate serious health crises. Malice, grudges, dwelling on past slights, cruelties and injustices are among the tensions that often cause, or worsen, high blood pressure, heart disorders and ulcers. ("It isn't what you eat that causes ulcers; it's what's eating you!") This is because man is neither a body nor a soul, but a soul that is using a body. When we entertain evil attitudes for a long enough period, they at last annoy and distress the body. Hatred is one of these evil attitudes. Hatred is a

137

vicious boomerang that, when thrown, gathers momentum and returns to injure the person who uses it, destroying his health and happiness.

Hatred may start as an occasional impulse, but it easily becomes an emotional habit. The hostile person seldom gives much thought to the significance of his feelings, his thoughts, his utterances. He has practiced the art of harsh faultfinding so long that expressions of violent dislike become automatic ways of releasing his own inner tensions and unhappiness. When his hostility is through with one target it sets up another, because hatred simply must express itself on something.

Hatred has been likened to alcoholism. When alcoholism seizes a man he will drink whiskey if it is available, or gin, or rum, and if nothing else is on hand, he will even drink wood alcohol. So, when a person gets the hatred habit, he will hate his real enemies, and then, when his hateful impulses remain unsatisfied, he reaches for other objects of hostility. He may become hypercritical of those near him, his wife, children, employers, employees, public servants. He belittles his neighbors and disparages the successes of his acquaintances. He reads wrong motives into the behavior of his associates and is slow to forgive them. He intimidates those he can and humiliates others. Those of other races, religions, nations and political parties supply him with hate objects. First he has the hate habit, then the hate has him.

Hatred begins in little ways, but how it grows!

Two thousand years ago Jesus taught that the world can be redeemed only through love. Twenty centuries have not eroded that truth. They have illustrated it and magnified it. And an age of nuclear weapons, conceived in hate and born in war, makes Christ's truth more apparent and imperative than ever. Once we were asked to be our brother's keeper. Now we have no choice. Once our Teacher was the kindly, loving Nazarene. Now our instructors are Nagasaki and Hiroshima. The clouds of atomic dust have faded over obliterated cities, but the lesson remains: hatred destroys individuals and nations; it ruins the hater as well as the hated.

Love or perish.

28

Life's Hidden Splendor

Just before dusk last evening my wife and I took a stroll through the lengthening shadows among the birches, hemlock and spruce that grace the land between our house and gate. We were looking for one of May's most winsome gifts to the world, wild violets.

A few steps off the trail we came to the grassy knolls where violets have flourished in other years. There they were again last night, violets in three hues: white blossoms as pure and delicate as a bride's veil, enchanting lavender petals that give the color violet its meaning and glory, and small flames of yellow that warm the month of May.

Many months ago the ancestors of these violets held wedge-shaped seeds in their pods. As the pods matured and dried, they shrank and finally burst, throwing seeds several feet away from the parent plant. There, where they fell, the seeds have slept, cradled among the roots of towering evergreens and gracile birches, blanketed by fallen needles and leaves. While the seeds slumbered, they

JAMES A. GARFIELD

changed from hard-shelled, unpromising, hopeless, life-less-looking things to tender sprouts and finally to blossom-bearing plants.

It is always with a feeling of mystery that I see the first spring violets and recall that one day they were unlikely-looking seeds, bearing not the slightest resemblance to the flowers now shyly nodding to spring breezes.

And what is so of violets is true of countless forms of plant life. Carrot, radish, and lettuce seeds look nothing like carrots, radishes, and lettuce. When you plant them in your garden you expect that the unpromising appearances of the seeds will prove deceptive, and beneath the death-mask life will faintly stir and finally burst its bonds.

The best things in life are seedlike. Wherever you find goodness and greatness, you can be certain there was a time when they did not look in the least like goodness and greatness. Once they were but seedlike possibilities,

141

small, unimpressive, with all the latent splendor hidden. God's good sometimes seems so little in a big world, so negligible, so hopelessly weak and inert, that we overlook it altogether, or refuse to put much faith in it. We recognize God's gifts only when they are plainly manifest, radiantly obvious and in full bloom.

This is especially true of people. We can often identify a good or a great person when he has achieved stature in the world, but how difficult it is to recognize such quality when it is still but a seed.

As a youngster Thomas Edison was told not to return to school because he was too stupid to learn. His schoolmaster described him as "addled" and declared that it was a waste of time to keep him in school. But Tom's mother believed in him, patiently taught and encouraged him, convinced that there were seeds of usefulness in him. And all the world has benefited from her faith in Thomas Edison's unfolded genius.

One spring day, some time before the Civil War, a lad came to the door of Worthy Taylor's farmhouse in Portage County, Ohio. The boy asked for work. Although he knew nothing about the lad, the farmer decided to take a chance on him and gave Jim a job doing general farm labor. Jim cut stove wood, brought the cows in from pasture, helped with milking and haying. He slept in the haymow.

As summer wore on, Jim fell in love with Taylor's daughter. But Worthy Taylor refused to let Jim marry her, pointing out that Jim was without money, without a name that commanded respect and without prospects of ever making a name for himself or a decent living. So Jim packed his few possessions and left the farm.

Worthy Taylor prospered and after the passage of thirty-five years tore down his barn to build a new and much bigger one. He then discovered on one of the haymow rafters that Jim had carved his name, "James A. Garfield." Jim was at that moment the President of the United States.

Keep faith in human possibilities under God. Many an unlikely looking lad near you is more than he appears to be. The future man is there; God's man to serve God's purposes in a needy world is there, even though veiled beneath a boyish swagger. Those possibilities deserve the homage of our meditative eyes and of our faith in what God can do with human seed. No "mere child" is "mere" in God's sight.

Furthermore, be trustful of what God can do with and through you. You don't think you amount to much? Neither did Christ's disciples feel they were of much account. Yet they were the seeds of future Christianity. Christ nurtured the incredibly small potential into miraculous power. They were like Marquis wheat, all the seeds of which, a few decades ago, could be held in your hand. But Marquis wheat now feeds the world.

When Napoleon was told that one of his projects was impossible, he replied in disdain, " 'Impossible!' That is not good French!" It isn't good religion either. One far greater than Napoleon told His followers, "With God all things are possible."

All the wonders God has wrought were once unpromising-appearing little beginnings.

29

Beyond Mere External Things

Colonel T. E. Lawrence, that intrepid adventurer who rallied Arabs to the Allied cause during the First World War, told of two desert chieftains who visited him in London after the war. The Arabs had saved Lawrence's life more than once, and "Lawrence of Arabia" was grateful to them. He invited them to England to see the sights. They stayed in the finest hotels. They were taken to the Tower of London and to Buckingham Palace and were received by King George and Queen Mary. Everywhere they went they were the center of attention because of their unusual garb and their association with Colonel Lawrence, a hero in England.

When the time arrived for their departure from England, Colonel Lawrence asked the chieftains to choose anything they wanted as a gift to take home with them. The Arabs went into serious, secret consultation. Then they announced that they had agreed on the gift they would most cherish. Of all the wonders they had seen they wanted most two hot-water faucets.

The Arabs did not understand that hot-water faucets alone will not furnish hot water. Hung on the walls of their desert tents the faucets would be merely ornamental, for behind hot-water faucets there must be plumbing, heating apparatus, and reservoirs of water, or the faucets will have little meaning. Can't you imagine Arabs transporting two faucets from London to the deserts of the Middle-East, hanging them on the walls of their tents and then squeezing and pounding them in fretful frustration because those faucets offer no water?

The Arabs are like the rest of us: we have too high a regard for the superficial. We are frequently unaware of the deep backing of resources every one of life's faucets must have. We have a great love for external things, and we glory in them. In education such externalism means getting diplomas and degrees without a sustained growth of knowledge and the enlarged awareness which the untutored mind misses; it means schooling without achieving an amplified usefulness. In marriage externalism means maintaining the appearances of wedded life but neglecting the soul of it, which is self-giving manifested in kindness, forgiveness, loyalty and companionship; it is ceremony without commitment, a faucet without resources. Externalism in parenthood means provision for all of a child's material needs and neglecting the cultivation of his spirit, furnishing a splendid house but a poor home, giving him good toys but dull table conversation, teaching a child to brush his teeth without inspiring him to brush his mind, training him to keep his body clean but not his soul. In religion externalism means following the rules but not the spirit; observing religious rituals, traditions and holy days without the wholehearted dedication of life to God which makes all else in religion meaningful.

People who best handle trouble when it comes are those

who have an abundance of spiritual resources behind the
walls of their lives. Their glory is not in faucets, but in
deep wells and vast reservoirs. When life makes heavy
demands upon their souls, when droughts arrive and the
world seems dismally dry and parched, they become re-
plenished and refreshed from sources Heaven has hidden
from the world. We all know such people. I do. A
few days ago a good friend of mine, a minister of the
gospel, died. His death came suddenly, without warning
to his wife, his children and the community that loved

him. Many who looked on as his family moved with quiet dignity through difficult days remarked about the stoical effort such splendid conduct must have demanded. Of course the bereaved wanted very much to carry their burden with good grace; therefore, will power and effort were involved. But these were not the secrets to the handling of their heartache. These people were not so much engaged in strenuous trying as they were in being hospitable to God. They knew that their grief was God's affair and that on the other side of human weakness lay the boundless expanses of God's strength. They recalled the great truths of their faith: God's dependable love; that ultimately His hands are in all things and all things are in His hands; the resurrection of their Lord, triumphant over death, as witness to the conviction that even death is not fatal to the souls of God's children. Behind the externals of their religion was a deep, abiding trust. They knew the meaning of resources as well as of faucets.

A New Testament benediction, written to the church at Ephesus, reads, "Now to him who by the power at work within us is able to do far more abundantly than all we ask or think, to him be glory in the church and in Christ Jesus to all generations, for ever and ever. Amen." This is the spiritual insight that goes beyond appearances: there is a Power, not of our own, working within all who are open to it and that Power is more abundant than our greatest need or our wildest guesses. There is a reservoir beyond the faucets.

The chief goal of life should be to make vital connection with it.

30

The Measure of a Man

Among the characteristics that distinguish human beings from the rest of the animal kingdom is the extent to which man is capable of distributing his concern, sympathy and love. A grizzly bear mother will imperil her life to protect her cubs. She will rush an armed hunter if she feels he threatens the welfare of her young. Even after being mortally wounded she will continue to defend her cubs. But a female grizzly will not hazard her life to protect the cubs of some other mother grizzly, nor those of a black bear mother, nor will she risk her life to guard the fawns of a neighborhood mule deer. Her concern is narrowly restricted.

Occasionally there are reports of a female dog with suckling pups adopting motherless baby skunks that are given her to nurse, and it is thought that some whitetail does will care for another doe's abandoned or orphaned fawn. But even in these exceptional, newsmaking instances, concern is narrowly restricted. The adopted in-

148

fants are not sought out, but forced upon the foster mothers, or else she chances upon forsaken youngsters, and an opportunity for expression of her natural instincts is ready-made.

But human beings, at their best, will seek out occasions for expressing sympathy, concern and love. And men and women have been known to lay down their lives voluntarily for total strangers and for people of other races.

One evening a professor of philosophy was about to go to work on his lectures for the following day and was tidying his desk before commencing his study. Among the papers he picked up was a magazine published by the Paris Missionary Society. He was about to throw the magazine aside when the title of an article caught his eye — "The Needs of the Congo Missions." The philosophy professor read the article, and then noted in his diary, "My search is over." The professor, Dr. Albert Schweitzer, had been seeking a place where he could invest his remaining years in some meaningful service to mankind, and the missionary report pointed to a place demanding a rare degree of consecration and hard work. Dr. Schweitzer began the study of medicine and surgery and went to French Equatorial Africa where he labors to this day. There this scholar, who has doctor's degrees in philosophy, theology, music and medicine, lovingly spends himself to bring healing to the bodies and minds of black men.

Early in life Albert Schweitzer demonstrated his expansive interest in humankind. As a boy he was healthy, rugged and strong, and he loved to wrestle with other boys who attended the village school. One day he threw a neighbor boy, and the youngster complained, "If I could have broth to eat every day as you do, I'd be so strong you couldn't throw me." Young Albert was so impressed that he went home and told his parents that as long as the neighbor boy could have no broth, he

would take none. He later discovered that other lads in the village were wearing old shoes that could not keep their feet warm. Albert's shoes were good, but he reported to his parents that he would not wear good shoes unless the other boys could have them. The Schweitzer boy was

150

a problem to his parents because he refused to live up to his social status. He preferred to identify himself with the poor and the needy.

Later in life he explained his philosophy of 'missions, saying, "If there is any ethical thinking at all among us, how can we refuse to let these new discoveries benefit those who, in distant lands, are subject to even greater physical distress than we are? . . . Whoever among us has, through personal experience, learned what pain and anxiety really are must help to insure that those who are out there in bodily need obtain the help which came to him. He belongs no more to himself alone; he has become the brother of all who suffer."

Sympathy, the capacity to suffer with and for other people, is one accurate index of character. The expansive, all-inclusive interest, concern and love that go out beyond the people who live under one's own roof are the measure of a man like Schweitzer. He is as big as the world is large.

How great is your concern? How far does your willingness to sacrifice time and money and energy go? How big are you?

31

Faces Beyond the Statistics

The power of imagination has been given a bad time by street-corner sages and park-bench philosophers. "He imagines things!" is a criticism that supposedly indicates that the subject is on the verge of lunacy. The person who makes a hobby of worrying or complaining is scoffed at, and we declare, "His trouble is all in his imagination." We have all known people whose imaginations brood over their neighbors, hatching out the vilest suspicions of what wicked deeds they are performing in secret and what evil motives prompt even their most innocent acts. Daydreaming and building of "castles in the air" seem like wasteful trifling to a world that idolizes efficiency, and we can hardly ridicule a person more cynically than to say of him, "He's a dreamer!"

But some of the best things that ever happen occur because someone's life is dominated by a vivid imagination. When it is controlled with reference to some worthy theme, imagination produces poetry, drama and novels, music, painting and sculpture, or it synthesizes a collection of facts into a scientific theory like Newton's hypothesis of gravitation, or it makes for invention like Edison's incandescent light bulb.

The good life, too, depends upon the noble uses of a vivid imagination, for goodness in social conduct involves a person's imagining he is in another's place. Without the capacity to sense another's fears and temptations, deprivations, disappointments, and griefs as our own, there could be no real sympathy in the world, for the very word "sympathy" literally means "to suffer with." Wherever sympathetic assistance is being rendered, wherever a great and unselfish service is being done, behind it all can be found someone's imagination, wholesomely engaged in feeling another's trouble as if it were his own.

One of the most powerful forces for good in the present century has been the American Friends Service Committee, an organization founded by Quakers to show their love and loyalty for their country and for offering their services to the world in every kind of philanthropic and charitable endeavor. Established in 1917, the organization has engaged the lives of unnumbered selfless people in relieving suffering around the globe. The chairman and moving spirit of the Committee during its formative years was Rufus Jones, a professor of philosophy, the world's best-known historian of mysticism, a writer, lecturer, and religious statesman. He was a personal friend of Herbert Hoover, and when, at the close of the First World War, the future President called for relief for starving German children, Rufus Jones organized help to the extent of twelve million dollars and for a time furnished a minimum of one meal each day to 1,200,000 German children.

The concern Rufus Jones felt for the world's needs was without religious, racial, or class boundaries. In December, 1938, Dr. Jones, then seventy-five years of age, sailed

for Germany with two Quaker associates. The purpose of
his voyage was to appeal to the German Gestapo to allow
the American Friends to give some relief to the persecuted
and suffering Jews of Germany. Emigration of the Jews
from Nazi Germany seemed imperative if any at all were
to avoid destruction, and no provision was being made for
the escape of these harassed and oppressed people. Finally
a few days before Christmas and after much maneuvering
Dr. Jones and his two friends were escorted into Gestapo
headquarters for a conference with deputies of Reinhard
Heydrich, feared throughout Central Europe as "the
hangman." There Rufus Jones presented a statement of
the purpose that had brought him and his friends to Ger-

many — to relieve human anguish. To assure the suspicious Nazis of the good intent of their American visitors he told how during the closing days of the First World War the American Friends Service Committee had directed the feeding of starving German children, and how they had brought coal into Vienna for the fires in the hospitals. He added, "We have simply, quietly, and in a friendly spirit endeavored to make life possible for those who are suffering. We do not ask who is to blame for the trouble that may exist or what has produced the sad situation. Our task is to support and save life and to suffer with those who are suffering." The result of this conference was that Quakers were allowed into Germany to oversee the expenditure of Quaker relief funds; Quakers were permitted to give aid to non-synagogue Jews who were not getting assistance from other organizations; Quakers were allowed to assist with the emigration of individual Jews from Germany — where to linger meant likely death. Rufus Jones and his friends had daringly faced forces of evil and offered them a way of love!

What was the secret of the effectiveness of this modern American saint? What made him spend so lavishly of his strength for countless thousands of other faiths and races he would never see? In large part the secret was this: he had a vivid and dedicated imagination. He never saw statistics concerning starving children overseas without seeing, too, hunger-pinched faces, hunger-bloated bellies, and toothpicklike arms and legs. As his biographer, Elizabeth Vining, said about him, "Rufus Jones saw always the human faces beyond the deadly statistics of need and he had the gift of making them vivid both to the workers and to the public to whom he appealed for support." That's it — seeing faces beyond statistics and then doing something about their need!

Would it not make a difference in our behavior if our imaginations were sharpened until we all saw faces beyond statistics?

Would we not do better in our treatment of the "backward" peoples of the world if we could imagine they are as sensitive as ourselves? Would we ruthlessly exploit them if we could feel their resentment as if it were our own? The millions of underprivileged of the underdeveloped areas in Asia, Africa, and Latin America are more than census statistics. They are people who think and wish and pray about an improved lot in life, about better agriculture, industry, education and health. Do we have the imagination to wish their wishes, dream their dreams and work for their welfare as if they were our own?

Would we not drive more carefully if, instead of knowing that nearly forty thousand people a year are killed in traffic "accidents" — and hundreds of thousands injured — we saw faces and bodies behind the statistics? Faces that stare up vacantly from blood-smeared pavements, faces with mouths that scream in pain, stony faces masked with mixed unbelief and grief — these are the faces behind the cold, unfeeling statistics.

But I need not go on. You can continue this thought and bring it to your own conclusion — in thoughtful, loving deeds. Whenever you see statistics on human need, look for the faces and sense the feelings behind them. Then do all you can to serve those needs.

Suppose that everyone did — how soon the world would change!

But even if only a few will "imagine things" in this fashion we will move a little farther in the direction of making a world brotherhood of our earthly neighborhood.

32

What It Means to Be Rich

One of the richest men in American history was John Muir, the naturalist. When in 1849, at eleven years of age, he arrived in this country from his native Dunbar, Scotland, John's family had little money, and when he died on Christmas Eve, 1914, his estate was not at all impressive. Nevertheless, John Muir was a rich man.

In 1899 Muir joined the Alaska scientific expedition sponsored by the fantastically wealthy American financier E. H. Harriman. One of the other travelers spoke enviously to Muir about Harriman's immense wealth. Muir replied, "Why, I am richer than Harriman. I have all the money I want, and he hasn't."

Muir's contentment with his financial lot was founded upon the knowledge that he was rich in other things besides money.

One of the ways in which John Muir was wealthy was in terms of time. He believed in taking hours to expose his eyes to beauty and to indulge his soul in leisurely conversation and fellowship with friends. He profoundly pitied the distinguished visitors who called upon him during his years in Yosemite, who were so time-poor that they could spare only one day among the beauties of the mountains and who rushed in and out of human contacts, never pausing to savor the spirit of a friend. Believing that people who travel fast see little of what they are passing, he one time set out on a thousand-mile walk from Wisconsin to the Gulf of Mexico, and all along the way he stopped to visit with children and old people, poor planters and well-to-do plantation owners, and to get acquainted with animals, birds, insects and trees, snakes and frogs, and any living thing that crossed his path.

Rich in courage, John Muir never carried a gun though he spent weeks at a time in the wilderness. He knew the flora of America so well that he was confident he could always find his food in the woods, and he was unafraid of any beast that walked. His courage was demonstrated, too, in the way he fought the timber barons and the mining interests which were denuding the Black Hills, the Big Horn Mountains, and the south California coast. When his cause of forest conservation was unpopular and the enemies of America's wildernesses were many and backed by big capital, the slender, ascetic-appearing naturalist struggled almost alone against them until others pitched into the battle and helped him. At last he won the preservation of vast tracts of wilderness as national parks.

John Muir was rich in faith. While he was not conventionally religious, he had a profound trust in God and in the dependability of the Creator's work. Once, after he had pointed out that glaciers were instruments in carving Yosemite Valley, a renowned but dogmatic geologist, Dr. Josiah Whitney, contradicted Muir's find-

JOHN MUIR

ings. Dr. Whitney denied that glaciers had anything to do with Yosemite and insisted that the floor of the valley had fallen in some prehistoric violent shaking of the earth's surface. At this John Muir snorted derisively, "The bottom never fell out of anything God made!"

The greatness of John Muir's attitude toward money was not that he abhorred wealth, but that he saw that money alone did not make a person rich. And this is the position taken by the great men of all time. Some people glibly quote the Bible to support their contentions that it is impossible for a person to be rich and at the same time spiritually minded. They quote Jesus' saying, "It is easier for a camel to go through the eye of a needle than for a rich man to enter into the kingdom of God." But they forget that He also said, "With God all things are possible." They remember His disappointment with the rich young ruler, but forget He praised one who wisely invested his money and said concerning him, "Well done, thou good and faithful servant." People think they are quoting the Bible when they say, "Money is the root of all evil." But at no place in the Bible is such a ludicrously untrue statement made. The Bible does say emphatically, "The *love* of money is the root of all evil." Some who have much money do not love it, but love the good things it can do, the wholesome benefits it can confer upon their community and world. Such wealth goes deeper than purses. It is soul-deep.

Again, there are people whose poverty is spirit-deep. They possess neither money nor an inner appreciation of the people near them, of the beauties that surround them, of the opportunities to do good that every new morning brings, of the good that is unrelated to stocks and bonds, bank accounts and real estate, dollars and cents, of the good that can be done with a warm smile, a kindly word and a helping hand. The rich can be rich or poor within. The moneyless person can be, too. The Bible does not oppose riches, but spiritual poverty. It does not denounce money, but it does condemn having nothing else but money and the things money can buy. It smiles approvingly on money as a good servant and frowns upon it as a tyrannical master. It condones having money in your purse and condemns having it in your heart.

Real poverty is not a matter of being moneyless. The poor of the world are the loveless, the thoughtless, the restless and hopeless, the joyless.

The world's richest people are those who have hearts full of love and peace and hope, minds full of high thoughts, memories packed with priceless experiences, and a record covered with gracious deeds.

33

Can You Laugh at Yourself?

One of the most dependable signs of spiritual maturity is the ability to laugh at oneself. Little children seldom possess this capacity. They are too self-centered. They can laugh at other children's ridiculous behavior, or they can laugh at themselves if the laughter seems complimentary, as when they have performed a clever trick. But to be laughed at because of small blunders or because of their appearance seems like cruel ridicule and they cannot join in it.

To see the ludicrous in oneself and to be amused, rather than tortured by it, is a mark of spiritual adulthood. And such a capacity is not common. The famed nineteenth-century cartoonist Thomas Nast entertained a group of his acquaintances one evening by drawing caricatures of each of the persons present. These exaggerated portraits were shown around. Each person readily recognized the caricatures of his friends, but many could not recognize the drawings of themselves. Of course not. To see clearly in ourselves what is comical, and to enjoy it, is a rather rare trait of character. Wherever it is found it signifies a touch of greatness.

One of the most likable men ever to occupy the White House in Washington was William Howard Taft. He loved people and was greatly loved in return by those who knew him best. Theodore Roosevelt one time said of him, "I think Taft has the most lovable personality I have ever come in contact with. . . . One loves him at first sight." Like most celebrated men, William Howard Taft was great only in spots. He had his share of faults. Sometimes it seemed that he hardly had a mind of his own. After succeeding Theodore Roosevelt in the White House, he tried to do everything his predecessor wanted done, afraid of displeasing or offending Roosevelt. He was timid, preferring to make people happy rather than angry even when important policies were at stake. His frequent lack of resourcefulness and imagination sometimes made him appear helpless in a trying situation. Once when he was on a public platform he was asked, "What would you advise a man to do who is out of a job and whose family is starving because he can't get work?" Taft replied in sincere puzzlement, "God knows. Such a man has my deepest sympathy."

But William Howard Taft was great enough to serve his country in many important positions, among them being Solicitor General of the United States, United States Circuit Judge of the Sixth District, a professor of law in two universities, Governor of the Philippine Islands, Secretary of War, President of the United States, and Chief Justice of the United States Supreme Court. And one of the traits that made him great was his ability to look at himself objectively — and laugh.

While occupying the eminent office of President of the United States of America, William Howard Taft never

allowed his pride of distinction to stifle his capacity to laugh at himself. He was fond of making fun of his enormous weight, which at one time reached 354 pounds, and he often told stories of how his mountainous flesh impressed acquaintances. One of his favorites was concerning a trip to New England where he enjoyed swimming in the Atlantic surf. A group of sun bathers was conversing on the beach when one suggested to the others, "Let's go in swimming."

"How can we?" asked one youngster in their midst. "The President is using the ocean."

Taft also liked to tell of a small boy whose habit of biting his fingernails worried his parents and fretted his nursemaid. The nursemaid, hoping to frighten the lad out of the habit, told him that if he did not stop he would swell up like a huge balloon and look ridiculous. The boy was impressed and broke his habit.

Some weeks after, William Howard Taft appeared at the boy's home for a luncheon engagement. The youngster entered the room, saw the huge man, marched up to him and exclaimed accusingly, "You bite your nails!"

Abraham Lincoln, like Taft, immensely enjoyed jokes at the expense of his personal appearance. He was fond of telling that in his circuit-riding days he was once confronted by a stranger who exclaimed, "Excuse me, sir, but I have an article in my possession that belongs to you."

The astonished Mr. Lincoln asked, "How is that?"

Taking a jackknife from his pocket, the stranger said, "Some years ago this knife was placed in my hands with the instruction that I was to keep it until I found a man uglier than myself. I have carried it from that day to this. Sir, allow me now to say that I think you are entitled to the knife."

This ability to laugh at oneself does not mean that all, or even most, aspects of one's life should be taken lightly. Great men look upon their moral failures with remorse rather than amusement. They indulge in rigorous and solemn self-accusation and in earnest repentance that leads to inner change. But they discern the difference between the tragic and the comical in themselves, and the ludicrous excites their wholehearted amusement.

What can laughing at yourself accomplish? For one thing, it can foster the habit of detached self-criticism. It is like enormous William Howard Taft looking upon himself as a fat fact, without excuses, apologies, or clever rationalizations. Ordinarily one would think that self-criticism comes first and laughter follows. But if one has developed little capacity for self-analysis he had better practice laughing at himself first, with the hope that self-criticism will follow in the wake of the forced act. It works — just as in a far more important realm the repeated act of praying for one's enemies as if they were loved results in loving them at long last.

Moreover, laughing at yourself makes you easier to live with. You will be less touchy. Your dignity will not be easily affronted. Those who wish to laugh at you can laugh *with* you rather than behind your back, and aloud and uninhibited, rather than half-strangled with fear they will offend you. Amusement at one's comical defects and funny foibles punctures ballooning self-righteousness and deflates egotism and self-conceit. Pomposity stands as much chance of survival in the midst of such laughter as does a balloon at a porcupine family reunion.

A noted psychologist of our time has said that a lack of humor is an outstanding characteristic of a large number of cases of psychological abnormality, and that in nearly all cases of insanity the sense of humor seems to be completely lacking. The insane person may show hectic gaiety, frenzied enthusiasm, and even may laugh hilariously, but never in humorous understanding of others or himself.

When I see dictators on the world stage, or lesser dictators in homes and shops, in clubs and offices, strutting their stuff, I'm inclined to pray that God might give them a little of that good grace that Taft and Lincoln had — the grace to look at oneself and laugh. Enough of it, spread thickly over humankind, might restore the world to sanity.

34

Next!

Not long ago there lived in Eagle Bridge, New York, a white-haired, thin wisp of a woman fondly known the country over as Grandma Moses. She was born in the wilds of Washington County, New York, on September 7th, 1860, and passed the century mark before she died. For most of her days she was a farm wife, busily helping with farm chores, raising five children (five others died in infancy) and performing the variety of cooking, baking, sewing, and house-cleaning tasks that befell a housewife before modern conveniences eased her load.

When she was almost eighty years old and so afflicted with rheumatism that she could no longer "do fancy work," Anna Mary Robertson Moses began to paint with oils as a hobby. When she had completed several pictures, admirers suggested that she place them on public display, so she had an exhibit in a drugstore, and another at a fair where she also displayed her fruit and jam. Grandma Moses won prizes at the fair for her canned goods, but none for her oil paintings.

However, Louis J. Caldor, a New York art collector, saw Grandma's drugstore exhibit, bought the paintings and asked for more. Exhibits in some of New York's most famous galleries and many more sales followed until Grandma Moses became nationally known.

One time after she had become widely known and her oil paintings had begun to command fancy prices Grandma Moses was featured in a radio interview. The interviewer asked the little old woman how it felt to be famous, with her paintings reproduced on millions of Christmas cards, and she remarked, "Oh, I don't think about fame much. I keep my mind on what I'm going to do next. I have got a lot of catching up to do!"

There is a touch of greatness in the simple wisdom of

Grandma Moses. Although most people have a desire for distinction, the wise do not seek fame as an all-absorbing goal; their work — what they are "going to do next" — gets the attention that the foolish give to public acclaim. Acclaim and applause to the ambitious are like salt water to the thirsty; the more one gets the more one wants. To care a great deal for fame necessitates caring less for more important things, because our span of caring is always limited.

One chief problem with craving the approval of others and seeking fame is that it divides one's attention between the thing one is doing and how that thing is going to be appreciated. And divided attention is a basic cause of misery (as can be understood by anyone who is trying to hear an address through the lusty squalls of the fussing youngster sitting two rows back; or by the person who is trying to concentrate on the concert pianist's rendition of a Chopin prelude while a bloodthirsty spring attempts to impale him through the upholstery of his concert-hall seat; or by the swain who at last has persuaded his sweetheart to take a boat ride where they can be alone, only to find they have been accompanied by a vast crowd of mosquitoes who sour the sweet-sounding love-talk with their villainous buzzing and their exasperating onslaughts on all exposed flesh). For full enjoyment of anything — oil painting, lecture, music, or romance — we need moments of undistracted attention. Grandma Moses knew that. She did not attempt to keep one eye on her painting and another on fame. When painting a picture, all her attention was on her work. And between paintings: "I don't think about fame much. I keep my mind on what I am going to paint next!"

This consciousness of the high value of the immediate occasion is a common denominator of greatness. The best people do not put off good living until the conditions are ideal. They know that one prepares best for tomorrow by living fully today. Alexander Graham Bell did not invent the telephone by dreaming of some distant time when the world would be interconnected by a communications system of his making. He had an immediate problem, a "next" thing to do which, in being done well, led him on toward designing the instrument that made him famous. It wasn't fame he sought, nor wealth, nor the telephone — at least not at first. Mr. Bell had been a teacher in a school for the deaf and while there he married one of his pupils. Later he began a series of experiments with electrical apparatus hoping he could devise an instrument that would help his young wife to hear. It was in that effort that Alexander Graham Bell invented the telephone, almost accidentally in the course of these experiments. The "next" thing was to help his beloved wife, and secondary matters, fame and fortune, came running after.

Robert Louis Stevenson's life was so plagued with pain, weakness, general invalidism, and the forebodings of death that he had to do his best with the immediate present if he was to be sure of doing anything at all. Moreover, his burdens were so great that he could hardly bear the thought of carrying them for long. The pricelessness of the present was vividly real for him. He once said:

"Anyone can carry his burden, however hard, until nightfall.

Anyone can do his work, however hard, for one day.

Anyone can live sweetly, patiently, lovingly, purely till the sun goes down.

And this is all that life really means."

Well, it may not be "all that life really means," but much of the meaning of existence lies in such wise handling of the immediate present.

Babe Ruth was one time asked what was the most thrilling moment of his career and he answered that it was during the third game of his last World Series. The Babe's game had not been going well. His team was behind, and it appeared the famous batsman would not be of much help to his teammates. Two strikes had been called on the Babe, and the disappointed crowd began to "boo" him unmercifully. The crowd's behavior both irritated and challenged him. Babe Ruth pointed to a distant spot and yelled at the jeering fans, "I'll knock it out there for you." And he did. It was the longest home run that had ever been hit at Chicago's Wrigley Field. The inquiring reporter asked the Babe what he was thinking about when that ball was pitched.

"What did I think about?" the champ snorted, "Why, what I always think about! . . . Just hittin' that ball."

Babe Ruth had the stuff of all champions: the capacity to concentrate on the present event.

While a painter like Grandma Moses, an inventor like Alexander Graham Bell, an invalid writer of adventure stories like Robert Louis Stevenson, or a baseball hero like Babe Ruth may illustrate, after a fashion, the value of attentiveness to the near-at-hand, the Supreme Example is Jesus Christ. Examine the Gospels and see how, though seeking to save the world, He began by redeeming those nearest Him. Indeed it was this tendency to help the "next" person rather than to be part of a fanciful, starry-eyed political revolution that disappointed His followers. They wanted a spectacular demonstration of His power. He should assume command of the multitudes, overthrow the Romans, and set up an earthly kingdom. Instead He associated with simple peasants and fisherfolk and showed them what they could be with His help. He dealt quietly with individuals — a woman of evil reputation who met Him at a well at Sychar, another woman about to be stoned for her sins, a crooked tax gatherer, a rich young ruler, a leader of His people who timidly came to Him at night, a dying thief on a cross next to His own. His life appears dramatic to us, but it was too commonplace to those who knew Him best, too colorless, too close to them, too familiar. He couldn't be the expected Saviour when He cared so little for spectacular things.

Had He been more dashing, or interested in glittering goals of conquest, power and fame, He would have satisfied His people better. He wanted a redeemed world, but He would not slight redemption of those near at hand by aiming at the redemption that was far off. So everyone near Him, the smallest as well as the greatest, the worst as well as the best, who would respond to Him felt His saving power.

Good occasions for service and spreading joy surround us all — now. Is there any better way of witnessing to our faith and helping God and man than by doing our best with what is nearest at hand?

35

In the Meantime

Now across America the amber hours of autumn swiftly pass. As the year rushes toward its close, farmers garner the last frost-crisped crops from the chilled earth. The fruits of the good land are harvested and heaped high in fields and baskets, wagons, trucks and bins. All that the vital seeds, the fertile earth, the kindly rains and the impartial sun could do this growing season has been done, and now before the yellow light of autumn fades away, a grateful people looks upon this bounty, one mighty harvest-basket, nation-wide and continent-deep; we breathe relief and murmur thanks.

Last spring this plenteous gift of Heaven was only a promise made by tiny seeds, rich fields and generous skies. Now it is man's sustaining food. What has happened between early spring and mid-autumn to make for this bounteous harvest? Obviously the farmer has been busy plowing, sowing, cultivating, reaping. Yet of all the hours that

have passed from spring until now he has spent only a small fraction of them on any crop. And of all the energy invested in the fruits of the earth, agricultural experts say that the energy of man and his machines represents only five percent; the rest comes from such natural sources as

174

sunlight and the earth's warmth. So what has man done?
He has worked, but mostly he has waited, hopefully, trust-
fully, believing that when he has done his best he can then
patiently abide nature's response. God's goodness, man's
effort, plus waiting is the formula for crops.

But the farmer's waiting is not *idle* waiting. He accomplishes what man can do while he waits for God to do what man can never do. Between sowing and harvesting, does he sit on his tractor all day, watching the fields for signs of life, fidgeting, nervously tapping his fingers on the steering wheel? Does he go along the rows of root crops, pulling up all his carrots and beets to see if they are thriving? Does he infest his days with worry and his nights with anxious sleeplessness? Of course not!

From the day he puts his seed spreader away until he hitches up his harvest machines, the farmer busies himself with such tasks as can be performed *in the meantime*. Are there cattle to be milked and fattened? Very well, he attends to these tasks. Is there hay to be cut and raked? He cuts and rakes it. Are there crops that mature early, before fall harvest, such as wheat, oats, rye and barley? Then he cuts, threshes, stores or sells them. The good husbandman must do much waiting, but he does not wait idly. He waits productively, creatively.

In the Bible waiting is never glum, helpless, hand-folding idleness. Nor is it simply a numb endurance while undergoing testing. "They that wait upon the Lord shall renew their strength; they shall mount up with wings as eagles; they shall run, and not be weary; and they shall walk, and not faint." So promised Isaiah the prophet (Isaiah 40:31). "They that wait" in the Bible will not be found sitting under a shade tree or dozing in a hammock while hoping for help from God. Nor will they be seen frantically pacing the floor, fretfully "sweating out" God's delayed answers to their pleas. Faithful waiting means trusting God will do for us what we cannot do for ourselves, and it also means filling the waiting-time with meaningful tasks. While Israelites waited for deliverance from their enemies, they attended to the fields that must be plowed, sown, cultivated, harvested. They herded, pastured and bred cattle, sheep and goats. Ships and nets were kept in good condition for fishing. Families were housed, clothed and fed. The welfare of the community was promoted. God would come to the aid of His people and deliver them from trouble. Exactly when, they did not know. But, in the meantime, there was much to be done. To God's people trustful waiting meant productive waiting.

Knowing how to wait is one of the secrets of living the life of faith.

Some people crave sleep and struggle for it. If it does not come within an hour they become panicky, provoked, or discouraged. The more they determine they must sleep, the more elusive sleep becomes. We cannot force ourselves to sleep, but we can pray for it, expect it and wait for it, and in the meantime do something worthwhile. Pick up a book and read. Make a list of the people who have blessed your life in the past year, some to whom you should speak some word of appreciation or send a note of thanks. Plan your next vacation. Sleep is like a butterfly: chase it and it flees from you; busy yourself doing something else and it may come and light upon your shoulder. While awaiting the blessing of sleep, do something worthwhile in the meantime.

Here is a woman whose husband, prominent in his community and a hero to his children, confesses that he has been unfaithful to his marriage vows. Both come seeking help to save their marriage. They are crushed emotionally and spiritually. She wants to know, "When will I again feel I can trust him?" "How can I wait out the weeks and the months until I am assured he loves me and will be true to me?" The husband wonders how he can endure the months ahead when he is severed from his illicit relationship and must let the wrong infatuation die. How can he bear the interval of waiting while he attempts to regain some trust and peace at home? Both

177

of these people have sought forgiveness for past wrongs done to each other. What now? The answer is that they must now wait for a healing of their deep wounds, but they must wait creatively and not idly.

Infidelity is less a symptom of physical sex wantonness than it is of deep self-doubt that seeks reassurance through sex conquest, or it is symptomatic of resentment that seeks revenge against the spouse. Since this is so, marriage partners need to spend some of their waiting time finding counsel and gaining insight into their urges that entice them into wrongdoing and into hurting each other.

While they are waiting they can practice being together at the times and places and under the circumstances that give them maximum enjoyment. They can plan surprising little deeds of thoughtfulness and consideration for each other and practice the courtesies that were present in their courtship and so easily forgotten in marriage. They can spend hours together in the places that strengthen and deepen their inner life, such as in worship. Spiritual healing, like physical healing, takes time, and the ill and the hurt must wait, and wait creatively.

One man of my acquaintance, who daily deals with pain from an incurable affliction, testifies that, while waiting for sedation to take effect, he studies difficult books in the fields of philosophy, science or history. He declares that this forces his pain into the background of his attention until powerful drugs can bring some relief.

Healing (both physical and moral), sleep and most other blessings come to us like autumn harvests, in due time and seldom with a rush. We all must learn to wait.

And trustful waiting is a glorious mixture of high expectation and significant action. It is being hopeful for the future and doing something that counts — in the meantime.

36

What Controls You?

Do you attempt to escape all difficulties and disliked duties, rather than face them?

Do you easily lose your temper?

Do you give in to your whims, buying merchandise impulsively rather than according to plan?

Do you follow your moods wherever they lead you, even into sullenness and sulky silence?

Do you fuss and fume over little things?

Do you frequently say and do things for which you are soon sorry?

Do you make many resolutions that are soon broken?

Do you tend to start many good projects that you do not finish?

Do you become grumpy and irritable when you lose a debate or a game?

If your honest answer to such questions is "yes," you have a control problem.

Self-control is one of life's first and most important lessons. A small child must learn to control himself if he is to fit into his social environment. He is soon taught that he cannot yank the tablecloth from the table no matter how much pleasure it gives him to watch the dishes clatter to the floor. He must not hit people who offend him. He must restrain himself from eating some things he craves, such as paper towels, crayons and the dog's rubber bone, and he must force himself to eat some foods he does not relish. Later, as respect for his body grows, a person learns to say "No thanks" to an offer of a second piece of pie or another dish of ice cream. He declines many invitations to late parties and denies himself all the excesses that make false promises of relief from boredom.

The mature person learns to be mannerly when he feels ill-mannered and kind when he feels unkind, and he is generous for the sake of good causes even when he feels a mite stingy.

Some measure of self-control toward other people is a stark necessity, or one becomes a social outcast, and if he does not control his physical appetites Nature casts him aside.

The writer of the New Testament letter, Titus, advises his correspondent, "Urge the younger men to control themselves" (Titus 2:6, RSV). Dr. James Moffatt translated the phrase, ". . . to be masters of themselves at all points." What alternatives are there to such self-control?

For one thing, if we cannot manage ourselves, outward circumstances will control us. An Olympic Games atmosphere crackles with tension and excitement, but a competing athlete dare not let the tumult get inside him and master him or he loses his event. Bobby Morrow won three gold medals at the 1956 Olympics. This tall sprinter with the nine-foot stride outran all others in the

100-meter dash, the 200-meter race and was on the American relay team that won the 400-meter race. Morrow later said that much of his success could be credited to the fact that he never "jumped" the starting gun. Officials enforce penalties for jumping the gun, and penalties mean the loss of a contest. Bobby's athletic skills would have been useless at the Olympics without his self-control expressed in patience.

We are all in danger of being controlled by circumstances, letting our surroundings master us. Teen-agers fall into moral looseness by becoming the slaves of circumstance, letting the excitement of a highly erotic society regulate their behavior, inducing them to jump the gun in sex experimentation before marriage. They penalize themselves.

Adults become slaves of circumstance and the victims of time and place. They are good in church, but look out for them in a business deal! They are well behaved at noon, and they misbehave at night. They may be gentlemen and ladies in a discussion held at their club, but dictatorial tyrants at the home dining table. They are all right in New Haven but all wrong in the night spots of New York. They are chameleonlike and get the color of their character from the environment. Circumstances control where there is no self-control.

There is a second danger: besides being mastered by the general circumstances around us, we are too easily controlled by other people's principles rather than by our own. We become *reactors*, rather than *actors*. We must see how others will behave toward us before we decide how we will behave toward them. If people are kind, we will be kind in return; and if they snub us, we will snub them. If they criticize us, we respond with criticism; and if they praise us, we answer with praise. This means we are lacking in self-control. Others control us.

181

A Quaker was asked why he treated a sullen, discourteous newsboy with such polite pleasantness. He replied, "Why should I let that fellow decide how I will act?" That Quaker's behavior is not controlled by other people's attitudes. He knows what sort of person he will be regardless of what those around him are like. He knows, too, the abiding principles worth standing for and how he should behave, no matter how unprincipled others are or how they misbehave. He has inner controls.

We are meant to be above the reptiles, amphibians and fishes which are "cold-blooded" creatures, their temperatures registering the temperature of their surroundings. We are "warm-blooded," with a constant temperature, no matter the weather. This is because the Creator has made us with inside regulators. And as far as character and behavior are concerned we are intended to be governed from within. As Paul said in writing to the Galatians, "It is no longer I who live, but Christ who lives in me: and the life I now live in the flesh I live by faith in the Son of God, who loved me and gave himself for me." Paul was self-controlled, and, in turn, the "self" was controlled by Christ.

What controls you?

37

On Having a Controlling Purpose

One secret of living with a minimum of fear, anxiety, and despondency is to have a worthy purpose. A good goal has magic qualities. It shrinks many a problem that seems too big to handle and causes petty concerns to vanish. When we believe that our purpose is of supreme importance, many temporary reverses and disappointments that fret aimless folk become secondary to us. The spot where we presently find ourselves may be uncomfortable, and even hazardous, but we know that our discomfort is less important than our aim and that where we are is not as important as where we are going.

During World War II, millions of newspaper readers were thrilled by the heroic stubbornness of little Jack Kelly. Jack was an English lad, eight years of age. Like many other English children he was evacuated from his homeland at the beginning of the war to escape the frightful German bombings of British cities. But on the way to America Jack's ship was torpedoed in mid-Atlantic.

The ship sank. Jack bobbed to the surface and clung to
some wreckage until he was picked up by three injured
survivors in a six-foot rubber raft.

What were the half-frozen eight-year-old's first words
when he was hauled into the raft? "I want my mother?"
"Who's going to take care of me now?" No. Jack's first
question was, "Which way is America?"

The question is a wise one. "Which way is my goal?"
When asked in a time of crisis such a question dispels
panic and controls fear. Mind you, I said it *controls* fear,
but it does not eliminate it. Attention to one's goal brings
fear under obedience to a person's main purpose. A Jack
Kelly will still be concerned about high waves filling the

rubber raft and may be apprehensive about how long it will take a ship to discover survivors of the tragedy, but all fears and anxieties are subservient to his strong intention of reaching America.

Isn't this always our problem, not to be utterly rid of fear, but to control it by some superior force? Fear is like fire, which is a splendid aid to man's comfort, warming his body, making his food palatable, smelting his ores into metals — when controlled. But fire is a terrible master, destroying man's forests, homes and man himself, when it rages unchecked by any other force. So fear of unnecessarily bringing harm to ourselves and to others may be incentive for driving carefully. Fear of disease may lead to sanitation and other good health practices. Fear of war makes for efforts toward peace. Controlled fear can have many wholesome uses.

A worthwhile purpose exercises such control over fear. For one thing, constant attention to the goal toward which a person is headed controls a fear of failure. This is true providing his purpose is high enough. Let us say that a person's goal is growth toward Christlike character. He will not need to fear that vexatious circumstances will thwart reaching his goal, for such a purpose is actually advanced by adverse circumstance. Every experience can add some measure of breadth and depth to such a life, especially unpleasant experience. The man of faith knows that he can use every hour for growth, as do trees, thriving on sunshine but also finding refreshment in rain and letting storms be incentives for developing deeper rootage. The faithful uses all kinds of spiritual weather for growing a soul. Tough duty stimulates diligence. Discouragement develops determination. Irritation tests temper and nourishes self-control. Every disappointment and misunderstanding suffered at the hands of one's fellows becomes a force for digging more deeply into human nature, enhancing compassion. Even blunders and sins teach a greater dependence upon God, so that failure leads to success in the quest for a more Christlike character. If character is one's goal, the purpose controls fear of failure.

Moreover, if our purpose is worthy, it will control fear of criticism. A circuit judge was plagued by a certain lawyer in a small town where the judge frequently held court. The lawyer was a man of vast conceit, felt he knew the law better than the man on the bench, and lost no opportunity to sneer at the judge's opinions and decisions. But the patient judge seemed never to be greatly annoyed at the lawyer's noisome manner. One time, after the lawyer had been particularly disrespectful, one of the judge's friends asked him at dinner why he did not reprimand the fellow for his rudeness. The judge answered, "In my home town there lives a widow. She owns a hound-dog which, on every moonlit night, barks at the moon all night long." Then the judge continued eating.

His friend asked, somewhat impatiently, "What's the point, Judge? What about the dog and the moon?"

"The moon keeps on shining," the judge answered.

History shows that the brighter some lives shine, the louder the critics bark. But the bright lives have kept on shining. If you have a radiant, God-given purpose, you will let it shine undistracted by fear of criticism.

Worthy purposes control our fears.

38

The Big Questions
What Do We Hate? and What Do We Love?

On Friday, November 22, 1963, in Dallas, Texas, a fatal encounter occurred between two men who were capable of tremendous hatred. One man was world renowned, the other obscure. The first man led a mighty nation, the other followed his lowest impulses. The nondescript, hateful malcontent, hiding high in a building overlooking the cavalcade of happy Americans, spotted his intended victim in the parade and fired a fatal shot into the vigorous body of the country's young President. The President collapsed and soon died without knowing who or what hit him.

President John Fitzgerald Kennedy and his slayer were both haters. The President hated war, brutal oppression, abject poverty and injustice wherever they were found. It was one of the aims of his life to destroy those evil influences which hurt men's bodies, cripple men's minds, and bruise men's souls. The sniper who shot the President was a hater, too. But he hated a man who symbol-

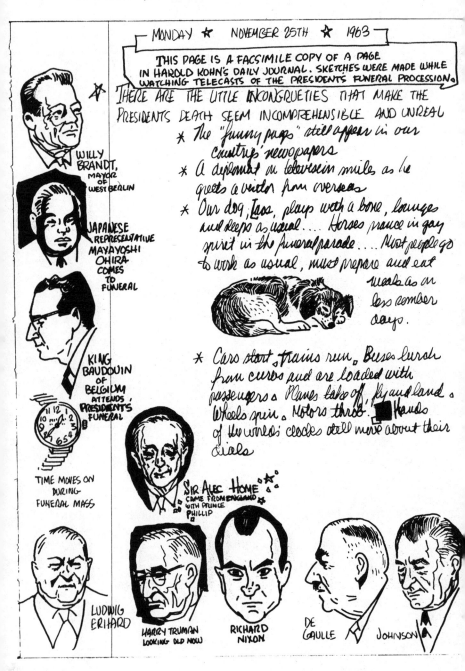

MONDAY ☆ NOVEMBER 25TH ☆ 1963

THIS PAGE IS A FACSIMILE COPY OF A PAGE IN HAROLD KOHN'S DAILY JOURNAL. SKETCHES WERE MADE WHILE WATCHING TELECASTS OF THE PRESIDENT'S FUNERAL PROCESSION.

THERE ARE THE LITTLE INCONGRUETIES THAT MAKE THE PRESIDENTS DEATH SEEM INCOMPREHENSIBLE AND UNREAL

* The "funny pages" still appear in our country's newspapers
* A diplomat on television smiles as he greets a visitor from overseas
* Our dog, Taos, plays with a bone, lounges and sleeps as usual.... Horses prance in gay spirit in the funeral parade.... Most people go to work as usual, must prepare and eat meals as on less somber days.

* Cars start, trains run, Buses lurch from curbs and are loaded with passengers. Planes take off, fly and land. Wheels spin. Motors throb. Hands of the world's clocks still move about their dials

WILLY BRANDT, MAYOR OF WEST BERLIN

JAPANESE REPRESENTATIVE MAYAYOSHI OHIRA COMES TO FUNERAL

KING BAUDOUIN OF BELGIUM ATTENDS PRESIDENT'S FUNERAL

TIME MOVES ON DURING FUNERAL MASS

SIR ALEC HOME CAME FROM ENGLAND WITH PRINCE PHILLIP

LUDWIG ERHARD

HARRY TRUMAN LOOKING OLD NOW

RICHARD NIXON

DE GAULLE

JOHNSON

ized high principles the assassin had been taught to despise. Both men hated. But John Kennedy's hatred was directed toward the world's evils, and his hatred supported and protected the things he loved. The assassin's hatred killed a man loved by millions across the globe, and this hatred made the world poorer.

"Hatred is something that should be banished from our lives," a well-known clergyman has said. I disagree. President Kennedy would have disagreed. The Bible disagrees. "The Lord loves those who hate evil," says the ancient Psalmist (Psalm 97:10). It is impossible to love without hating. Love and hatred go together, like opposite sides of the same coin. Men who love health must abhor disease. Those who love law and order must detest anarchy and criminality. If we love freedom we will loathe tyranny; if we love equality of opportunity we will be revolted by oppression; if we love peace we will hate war. There is a world of difference between a sniper hating a man, aiming to destroy him, and a gallant President despising oppression wherever he found it and resolving to throw all the powers of his personality and his high office against it. At Dallas the two haters had a brief, long-range encounter. The President died. A few hours later the assassin himself was assassinated. Now the man whose hatred was misdirected is lamented by few, while the one who knew how to direct his passionate hostility for the sake of all humanity is missed and mourned by the entire civilized world.

The evil in hatred is not in possessing it but in misdirecting it. We sin when we hate those who disagree with us, or those who hurt us. Furthermore, when we hate people we grant them incalculable power over us. Our hostility toward them permits them to rule over our sleep, raise our blood pressure, spoil our appetite and control our happiness. When we hate a person we blind ourselves to his sorrows and sufferings and virtues. Thus we impair our own insight and understanding and work destruction upon the higher sensibilities of our natures. But when we love God's children and hate the evils that hurt them we are properly motivated to use our powers and skills to help God improve His world.

Could it be that someday, under God's guidance, the world's peoples who wept at the news of the President's death may learn to follow the example of the slain leader rather than that of his assassin, may learn to hate and destroy evil rather than each other? May it be that we shall learn to employ our vast resources to strike out poverty, expunge disease and erase from the earth cold brutality, the searing scourge of war and our terrible fear of each other?

We cannot rid the world of hatred, as we have so often been advised to do since the awful event of November 22, 1963. We should not if we could. Love and hatred are in the world to stay as long as man remains here. But each of us has an awesome choice to make. We must either love evil and hate good or love good and hate evil. Moreover, we must learn to identify good and evil when we see them.

Will we dedicate ourselves, as did the President's slayer, to those things that destroy the best in man, or will we consecrate ourselves, as did the President, to what will support the welfare of man? The world's big questions now are not, "Do we hate?" or "Do we love?" but "What do we hate?" and "What do we love?"

39

The Poetic Spirit

Not long ago Robert Frost, America's unofficial poet laureate died. He was eighty-eight years of age when a blood clot in the lungs took him. All America, and much of the civilized world, mourned Frost's passing.

Robert Frost was a strange mixture of a man, granite compounded with gentleness, simplicity stirred into profundity, and a bitter-sweetness that flavored much that he said to the world.

He wrote in a plain, roughhewn style about everyday things, about the land, and good fences, and stone walls, about swinging on birches and scuffing through fallen autumn leaves, about horseback riding and blueberrying, and "stopping by woods on a snowy evening." To all common experience he gave uncommon expression.

Although Robert Frost has gone from our midst, his influence lingers. We need what he had to say about the mystery surrounding our everyday lives. He still appeals to our capacity for delight in simple things and our won-

der at commonplace things. Above all else, he shows us what it means to see life in a poetic fashion.

The one distinguishing mark of the poetic soul is his ability to respond to ordinary things with extraordinary wonder. It doesn't take much of a man to be astonished and contemplate about an earthquake or the eruption of a volcano. But to find rich meaning in a "tree at my window" which Frost saw every day, without becoming numb to its presence — that takes poetic feeling. It takes a reverent man to discover some universal meaning and to make poetry out of a New Englander's experience of mending fences and to make world famous a simple line like

Something there is that doesn't love a wall.

A rare eclipse of the sun excites wonder in any man who watches. But the reverent man, the poet and the philosopher are awed by every morning's sunrise and each evening's sunset. Robert Frost would have felt at home with Edward Dickinson (father of the poetess Emily), who once rang the church bell in Amherst, Massachusetts, as if to summon the town's people to help fight a fire. The whole town came running, but when they arrived at the church, they found Dickinson only wished to call attention to the sunset. Small wonder that Dickinson's daughter wrote poetry after being exposed to a soul like that.

Every poet, and Robert Frost especially, has engaged in such bell-ringing. Every good poem aims to call our attention to something significant that we are likely to miss.

We need a lot of such bell-ringing in our world, and we need a lot of people who will run to see the sunsets.

40

We Belong to Each Other.

One day an elderly lady who owns a large country estate asked me to advise her as to where she should plant pine, cedar, and maple on her land. Knowing of my interest in nature, she shared with me her concern that the land would be a place of arboreal beauty for many years to come. She explained, "I shall never see these trees mature, but someone in the future will enjoy them." Long after her passing, patterns of light and shade will adorn the earth; the music of whispering needles and leaves will be performed by playful breezes; the rich, black topsoil will be saved from erosion by the protective embrace of countless roots and rootlets. Someone's future will be brighter because of the thoughtfulness of this good woman.

This gracious lady has mastered one of life's most meaningful secrets: she has learned how to let her interests and joys reach out and serve the good of people she will never see. She is aware of the joint membership she holds in life with people unknown to her, and she has

194

formed a significant fellowship with generations beyond her. She has thought of them, planned for them, worked for them. Her love of beauty is being shared with them, and the joy she finds in trees will be spread to them. By planting small trees now she is communicating across the years with some people who may not arrive in the world for another hundred or two hundred years. She is saying to them, "Please stop a while. Rest. Look. Trees count. And you count. Long before you were born someone thought of you and your need of beauty and shade."

Such a wholesome attitude toward people who are outside our circle of close friends and relatives is basic to religious living. We humans belong to each other. We are important to each other, not only as far as marriage and the family are concerned, not only as far as employers and employees or the linkages between neighbors in small communities are concerned, but all people of all generations belong to each other. God has so fashioned the world that the effects of any one person go out from him in ever-widening circles to families, races, religions and generations other than his own. The Apostle Paul, while preaching to the Athenians, spoke of the essential unity of mankind, saying of God, "He made of *one* every nation of men to dwell on the face of the earth." The King James translators rendered this passage, "He . . . hath made of one blood all nations of men." All translators agree Paul was speaking of man's kinship under the Fatherhood of God; we belong to one another because we belong to the same Father.

Our connections with each other make it inevitable that, for good or evil, others will feel our influence whether we wish it or not. We bear traces of good and evil that have come to us from unseen and unknown persons; and others, unseen and unknown to us, will feel the effects of our lives. If we have gained good fortune without hard

195

work and without suffering, it is because someone else has worked strenuously and suffered before us. If we labor industriously and suffer without apparent reward, it is so that others can prosper from our work and trouble. When we are at our best, all the world is a little better for it. When we do wrong, the world is somewhat worse for it.

196

We all have some power for making our lives felt in other lives.

A chief difference between the responsible person of faith and the irresponsible person is that the former is constantly aware of the importance of his influence and is thus *intentionally* influential, while the latter is influential, too, but accidentally, impulsively, or from poor motivation. The good man *invests* his influence, while the mediocre man *squanders* his. And, since the good man knows his influence and responsibility do not end with his family, neighborhood, race, religion or generation, he does all the good he can regardless of such secondary considerations.

Dr. Wilfred Grenfell, the famed medical missionary to Labrador, once called upon a woman who suffered from tuberculosis of the ankle, and the doctor found it necessary to amputate her leg. A short time later the great doctor made a brief lecture tour of the United States and, while speaking in a Congregational church, asked if anyone knew of a person who might donate an artificial leg to the needy Labrador woman. At the close of the meeting a Methodist woman told the doctor that her husband, a Presbyterian, had died and left a wooden leg in good condition. Dr. Grenfell accepted the gift of the leg and later fitted it to the native of Labrador. He said, "When I, an Episcopalian, took that Presbyterian leg, given to me by a Methodist in a Congregational church, back to Labrador, it fitted my Roman Catholic friend, and she could walk."

We belong to each other; all men everywhere do. What we possess in the way of goods and compassion and grace fits someone's needs. The healing of the world's social, economic and spiritual ailments rests upon our recognition of this truth that we who belong to the same God belong to one another.

41

Made from Driftwood

A table lamp for which I have a special fondness stands in my study. It was given to me as a token of friendship by a ten-year-old boy who suffered from a mortal illness. One night near the end of his troubles, while I stood at his bedside, he whispered secret instructions to his grandfather, who went to a back room, returned with a lovely lamp, placed it in my hands, and said, "Woody wants you to have this." A few days after I received the gift, Woody died.

Nearly five years have passed since I spent that evening at the dying boy's side. The lamp still stands near my desk, treasured because it is a magnificent memorandum of two things. First, the lamp reminds me of Woody, a dear boy, unspoiled, although he was the only child of his parents and the last male descendant on both sides of his family. He was a lad of rare tenderness and thoughtfulness, unusually appreciative and uncommonly courageous. Even while in extreme pain he thought of

others. When I see the lamp, I remember Woody's unselfish good nature.

Secondly, the lamp with the driftwood base is a reminder of one of the basic truths of the Christian faith:
every castoff, discarded thing has possibilities beyond our
wildest imagination. Woody and his grandfather had
found this piece of grayish-brown driftwood while strolling
along the beach of one of America's largest inland lakes,
Lake Michigan. It was of little use the way it was. But
they took it home to the grandfather's workshop where it
was fashioned into an attractive lamp base, then wired.
They made a shade for it, and finally Woody gave it to me
his friend. It stands near me now as a steady reminder that
some of the loveliest and most useful things in life are
created from discards and forsaken things. Some of the
best things are made from driftwood found along the shore.

So the lamp is a symbol of salvation, one of the chief
functions of the Christian faith. "Salvation" is an old-
fashioned religious word that should never have lost its
currency and its exciting original meaning. "Salvation"

comes from the same root as the word "salvage," meaning that which is rescued from wreckage, fire or trash-heap. The word evokes memories of driftwood saved from the ravages of sand, water and insects on the lake shore or sea beach, of ships and their cargoes being rescued after a disabling storm, of a house and its furniture being restored after a fire, of works of art that have arisen from discarded materials.

Michelangelo, perhaps the supreme artist of the Italian Renaissance, one time salvaged a huge block of marble that Donatello had rejected because it was imperfect. From it he carved the noble and majestic "David," a piece of statuary with a grandeur seldom excelled in the history of the fine arts.

Belief in salvaging, or salvation, is elemental to Christian faith. Read through the Gospels, and see what was Christ's first response to those people who were thought by society to be of little worth. While some saw the outcasts just as they were, Jesus looked them over, and looked them through and through, and gauged them in terms of what they could become by God's grace.

Thus, a castoff, driftwoodlike woman of unsavory character and reputation became one of the select few who remained faithfully near to Him at His crucifixion, and visited His tomb on the first Easter morning.

Matthew, a slightly crooked taxgatherer, become a disciple, and the changeable, tempestuous Simon became Saint Peter, who helped establish the Church and was a martyr for Christ's cause.

When Jesus found people, they were often what the world would call "good-for-nothings," but after He had reclaimed them, they became useful to God and man. They were salvaged, reclaimed into something of greater worth than they could ever have become by their own efforts alone.

Wouldn't we all live happier, more useful lives if we developed and maintained Christ's holy habit of seeing people not only as they are, but what they can become, with God's help?

And wouldn't we all be spared utter discouragement with ourselves and despondency over our worth, if we would keep in mind that Christ is the world's foremost Craftsman and can always make of any willing piece of driftwood a bright and shining thing?

42

Things That Crumble and Things That Last

When I was a little lad I loved to watch my father mix concrete. He had been a carpenter in his youth and always retained his liking for building. He constructed our garage, remodeled our house, laid a new floor in our basement and laid new sidewalks where they were needed on our lot. Always there seemed to be some concrete work to do. Trucks moved into our driveway, hauling gravel, sand, and bags of cement. Dad then attached the garden hose to an outside faucet for a plentiful water supply, and he brought the big sieve out of storage. This sieve he had built from screen mesh nailed to a wooden frame. Then Dad sometimes let me shake the sieve while he poured gravel onto it. All the little particles fell through the mesh and into the mixing tub while the bigger pebbles remained on top of the screen, separated from the rest of the material. Dad then mixed the fine gravel with the sand and cement and with water from the garden hose, thus forming the concrete he needed for sidewalks, basement or garage floor.

When an earthquake hit Alaska on Good Friday, 1964, I remembered shaking that sieve and seeing the little grains of gravel disappear beneath the screen and the larger ones remaining upon it. Good Friday's disastrous earthquake in 1964 destroyed houses, demolished business-es and split schools in two in Anchorage, almost ex-tinguished nearby Seward, brought havoc to Kodiak and to a town as far away as Crescent, California. Railroad tracks were twisted, gas pipes, water mains and power lines were broken. Worst of all, many lives were lost.

Nevertheless, today's tides will ebb and flow; today's sun and tonight's stars will shine in Alaska and Cali-fornia, as well as elsewhere. The seasons will continue to change from winter to mild springtime and sunny summer, to mellow, ripe autumn and back to winter again. Before the first man appeared in Alaska or California, earthquakes shook the western edge of the continent. The earth opened in mighty cracks. Trees fell. Boulders thun-dered down the mountain sides. Some creatures died. But the sun and stars still illumined the turbulent earth and the seasons continued their unceasing coming and going. There are some things that outlast earth's rapid changes.

203

The writer of the New Testament book of Hebrews may have known nothing about making concrete, but he knew well the principle upon which a sieve works. Perhaps he had lived through an earthquake: his language seems to show an appreciation for such a terror. He told of how God had promised His people, " 'Yet once more I will shake not only the earth but also the heaven.' This phrase 'Yet once more' indicates the removal of what is shaken, as of what has been made, in order that what cannot be shaken may remain."

When our world is badly shaken we can count on some things remaining secure. For one thing, there will always remain some discernible order in nature. We can count on that. This world is not haphazard, but designed — constructed with an organization that reaches from this tiny earth to the farthest star. The more scientists have penetrated the secrets of the natural world, the more order they have discovered. Weather, once thought to be capricious, is becoming more and more predictable as its patterns are revealed. Once the paths of tornadoes were thought to be purely random, but now their courses are plotted with considerable accuracy. More than likely, before long, when man's knowledge has advanced apace and his instruments of detection are more sensitive, earthquakes will be precisely forecast as to time, location and strength. This order which scientists have discovered and upon which they depend the man of faith interprets as evidence of God's dependability and trustworthiness. This order remains above earth's shattering changes.

As long as man remains here this, too, will remain: man's seeking for something before which he can bow, something that will command his life and which he can trust. When a man has found that something, it will always become his Absolute, his God, whether it is money, security, popularity, fame, the state, or the Supreme Goodness revealed through Jesus Christ. No disaster has ever put an end to man's persistent seeking for an authority, power and goodness that transcend his own. Instead, trouble heightens the earnestness of the search. Man's craving for God remains unshaken after every convulsive event.

And God, the Answer to man's heart-hunger, still lives. Arthur Hugh Clough, a minor nineteenth-century English poet, cited a major truth after having lived through turbulent times. He watched the awesome clash of nations at war, the awful devastation wrought by the truculence of man and the afflictions of nature. His life was plagued by uncertainties. Nevertheless he prayed,

> *It fortifies my soul to know*
> *That though I perish, Truth is so:*
> *That howsoe'er I stray and range,*
> *Whate'er I do, Thou dost not change.*
> *I steadier step when I recall,*
> *That, if I slip, Thou dost not fall.*

God still lives. He is unshaken, unfrightened. He has plans and is competent and in charge of things.

Trouble shakes us like a sieve, and earth's events jolt us like an earthquake. But such unsettling agitations are revelations. They disclose the values that last — the essential order above life's seeming disorder, man's abiding need for God and God's everlasting readiness to rescue and redeem man.